Tracing for Toddlers

Learn to trace lines, shapes, letters and numbers.

This book belongs to:

....

....

This book is gradually structured beginning with line and shape tracing and transitioning to letters and numbers.
This pre-handwriting workbook will help your toddler make their first step towards the fun world of tracing.

To encourage writing development, guidance from a parent, caregiver, or teacher is necessary.

© Copyright 2021 - All rights reserved.

You may not reproduce, duplicate or send the contents of this book without direct written permission from the author. You cannot hereby despite any circumstance blame the publisher or hold him or her to legal responsibility for any reparation, compensations, or monetary forfeiture owing to the information included herein, either in a direct or an indirect way.

Legal Notice: This book has copyright protection. You can use the book for personal purposes. You should not sell, use, alter, distribute, quote, take excerpts, or paraphrase in part or whole the material contained in this book without obtaining the permission of the author first.

Disclaimer Notice: You must take note that the information in this document is for casual reading and entertainment purposes only.
We have made every attempt to provide accurate, up-to-date, and reliable information. We do not express or imply guarantees of any kind. The persons who read admit that the writer is not occupied in giving legal, financial, medical, or other advice. We put this book content by sourcing various places.

Please consult a licensed professional before you try any techniques shown in this book. By going through this document, the book lover comes to an agreement that under no situation is the author accountable for any forfeiture, direct or indirect, which they may incur because of the use of material contained in this document, including, but not limited to, — errors, omissions, or inaccuracies.

PART 1
TRACING LINES AND SHAPES

Trace with your finger and then with a crayon.

Start at ①

Follow the dotted line.

End at the arrowhead ▶

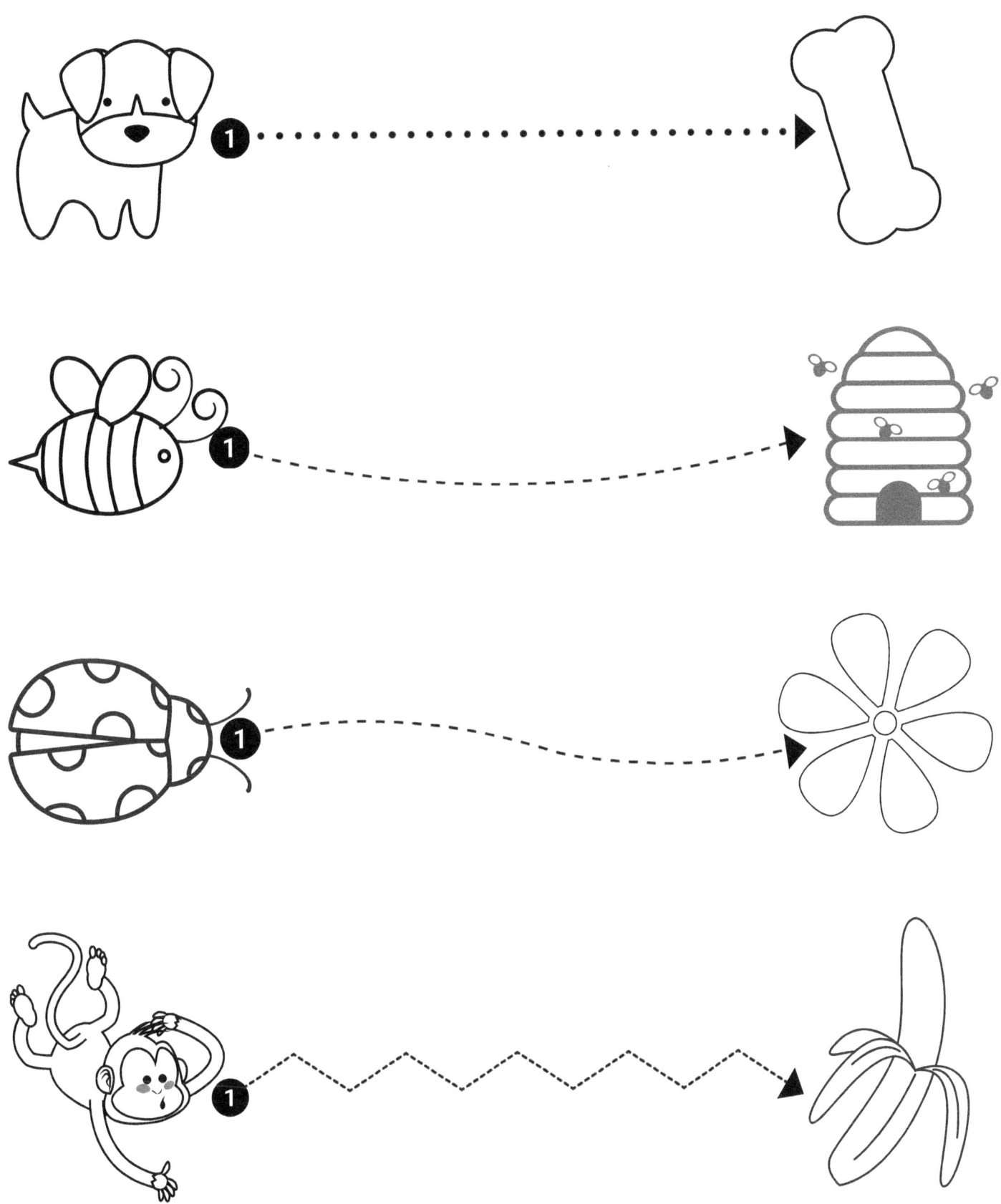

CIRCLE

Let's exercise the circle a little bit more!

SQUARE

Let's exercise the square a little bit more!

TRIANGLE

Let's exercise the triangle a little bit more!

STAR

Let's exercise the star a little bit more!

RHOMBUS

Let's exercise the rhombus a little bit more!

PART 2
LETTERS

Trace with your finger and then with a crayon.

Start at **1**

Follow the dotted line.

End at the arrowhead

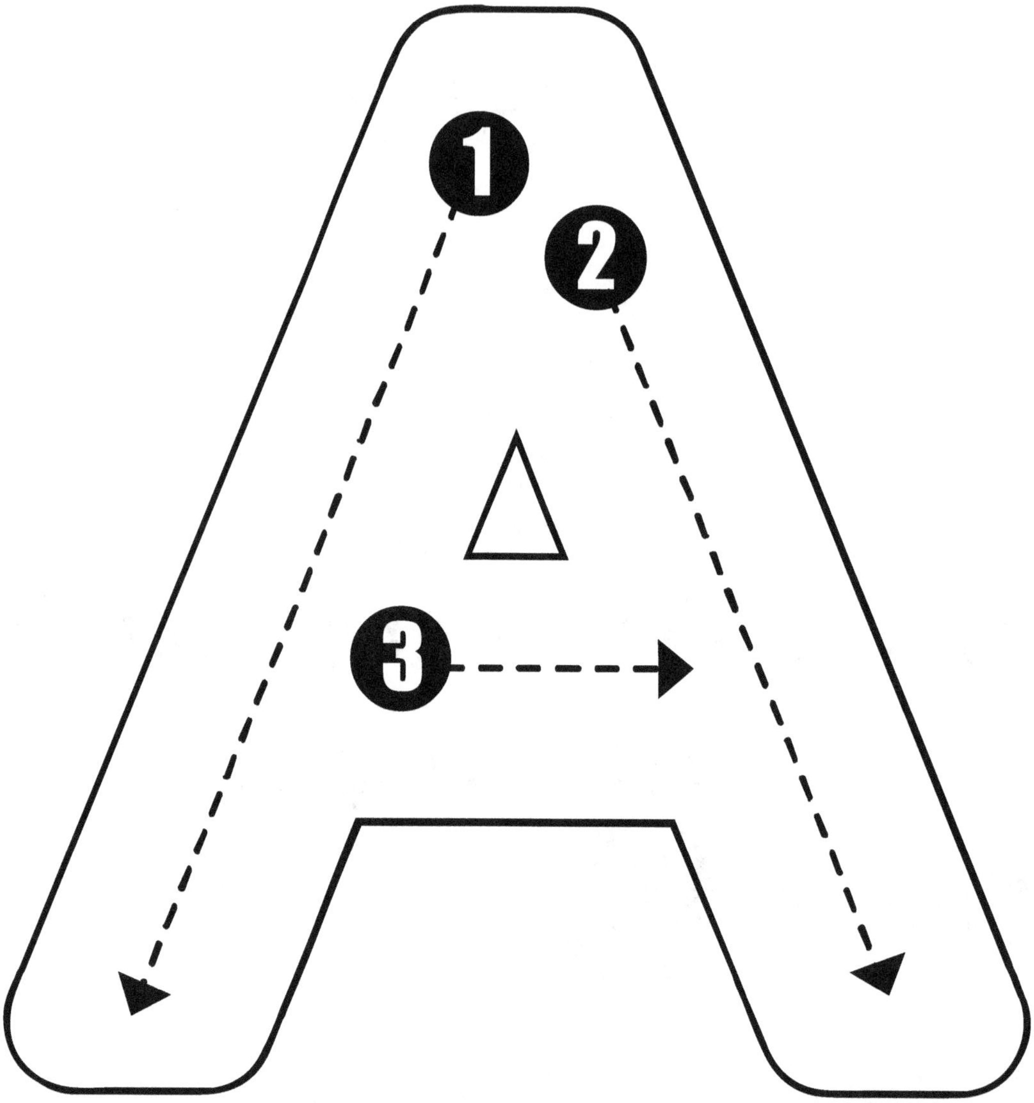

ANT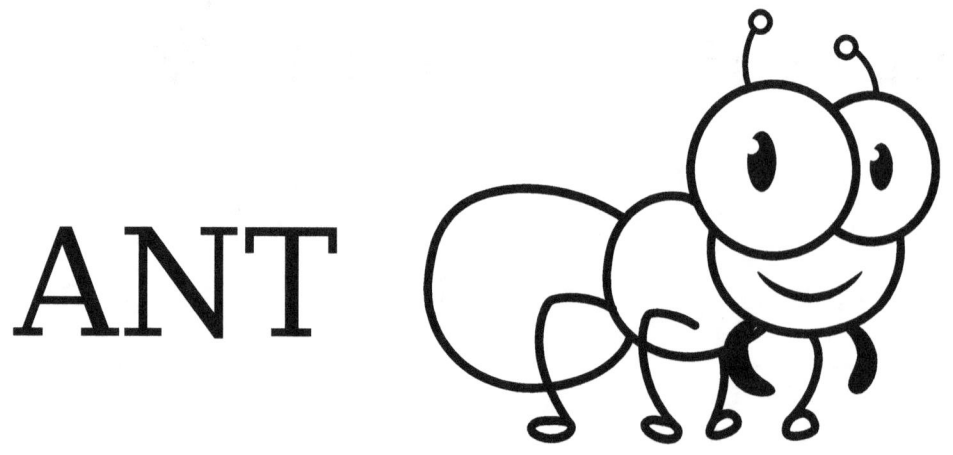

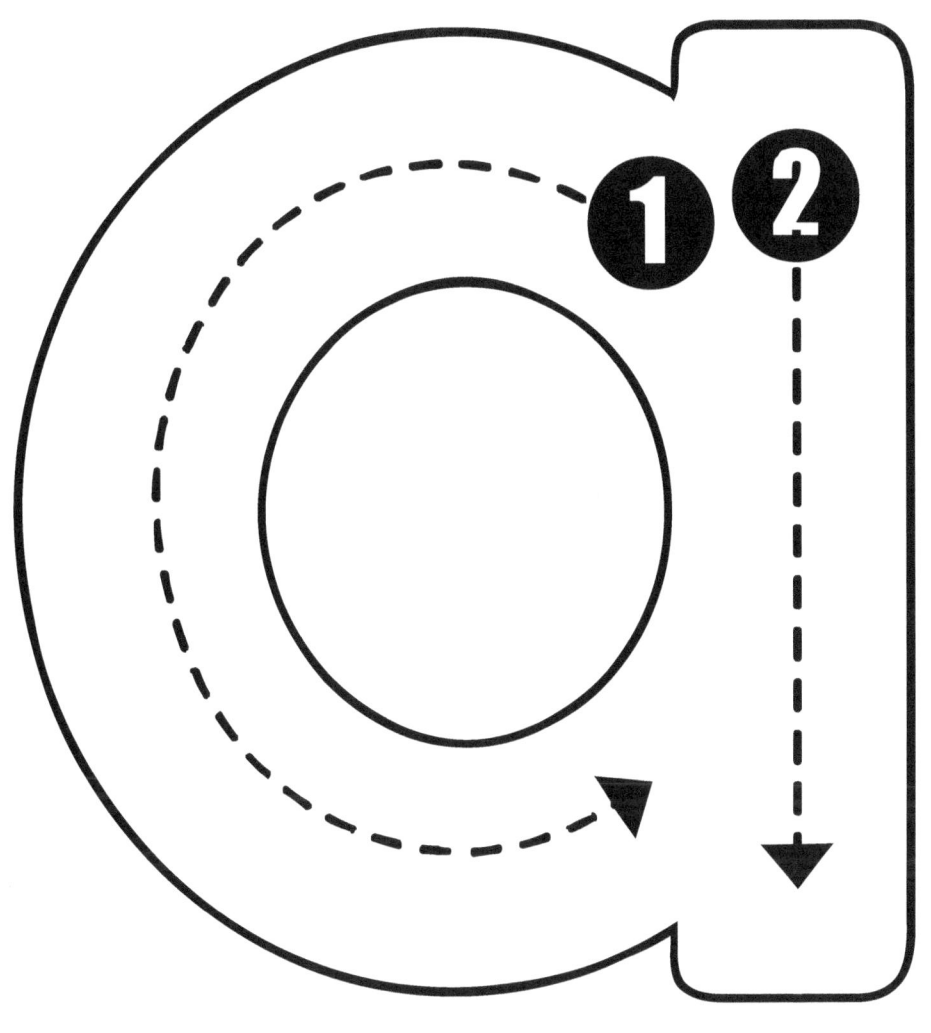

ant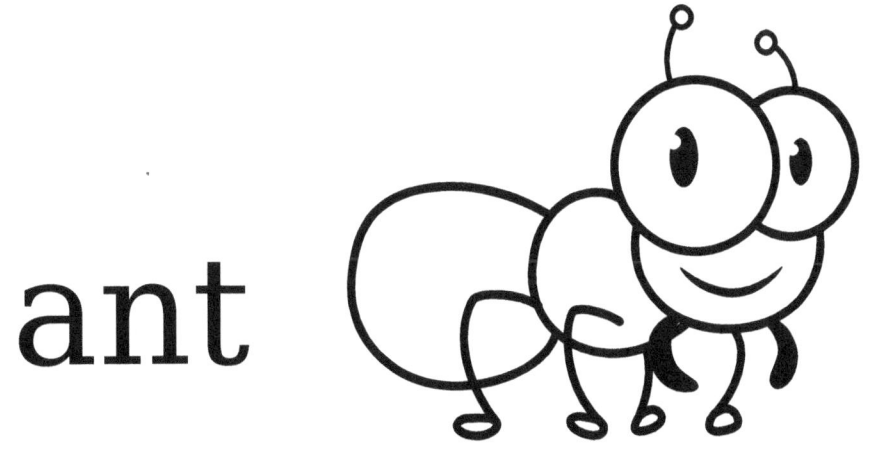

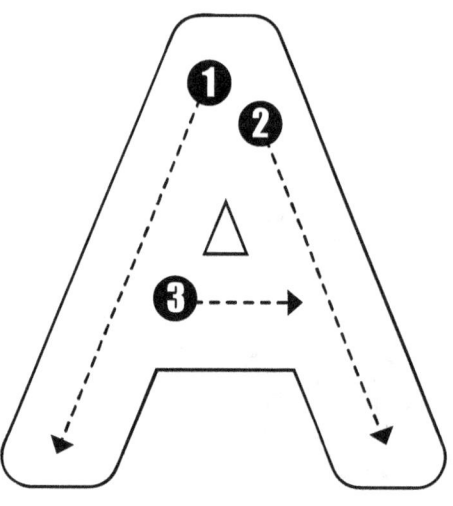 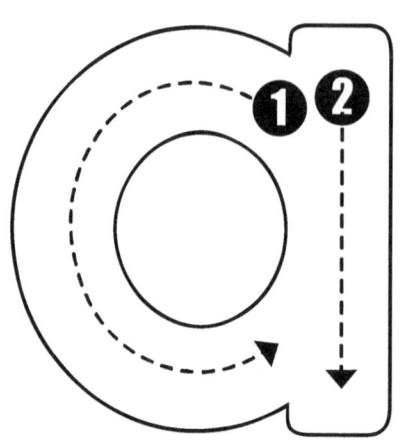

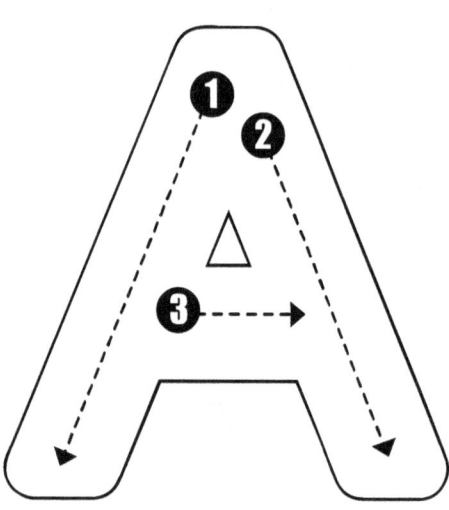 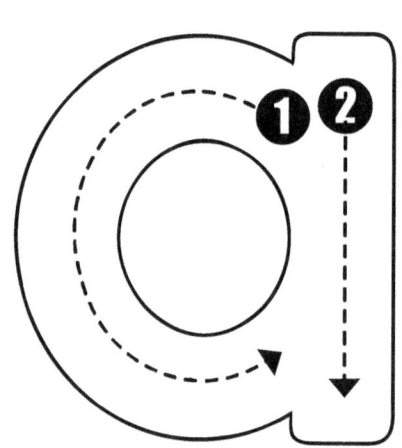

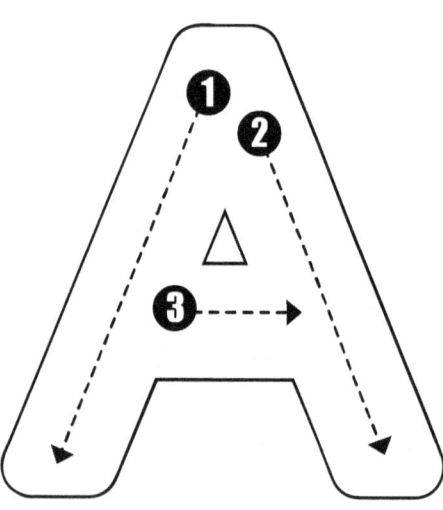 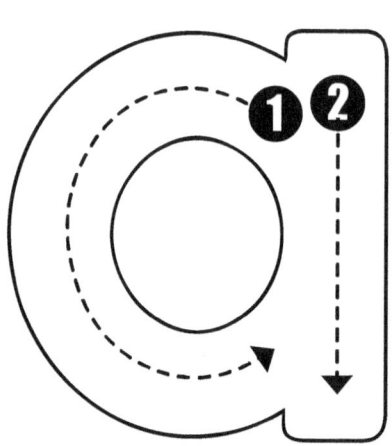

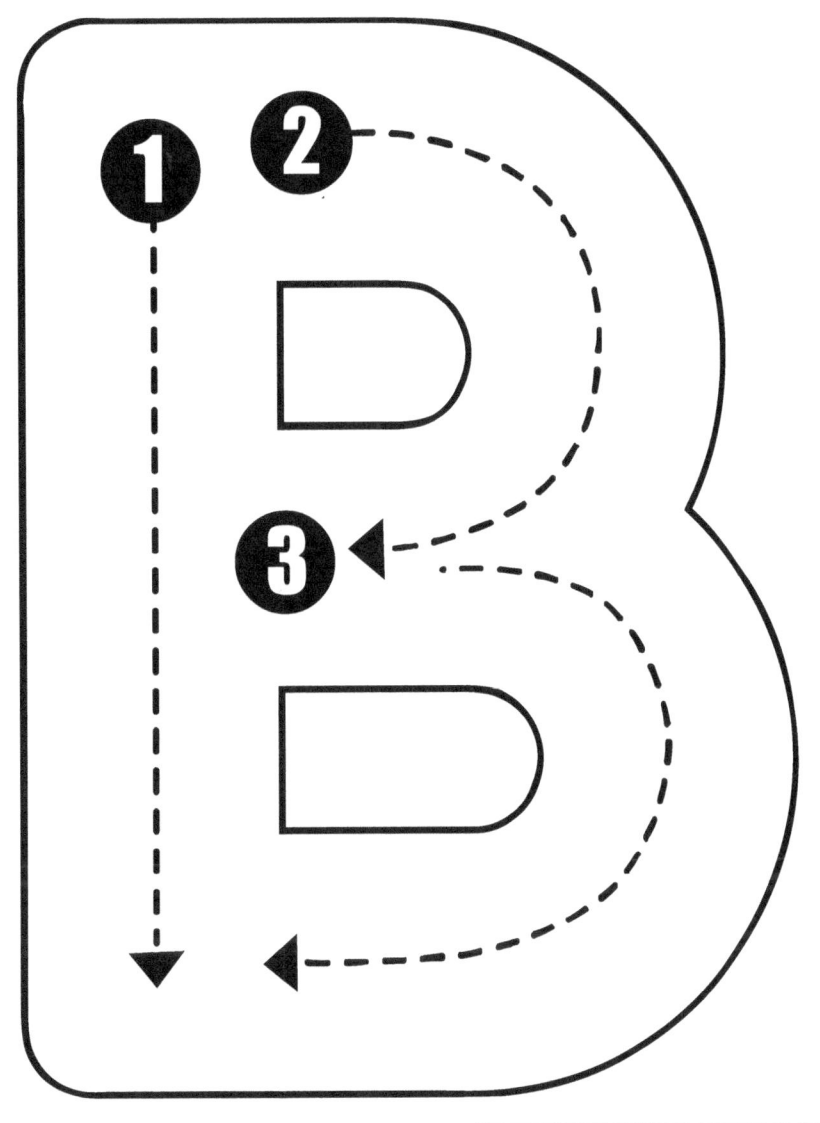

BEE

bee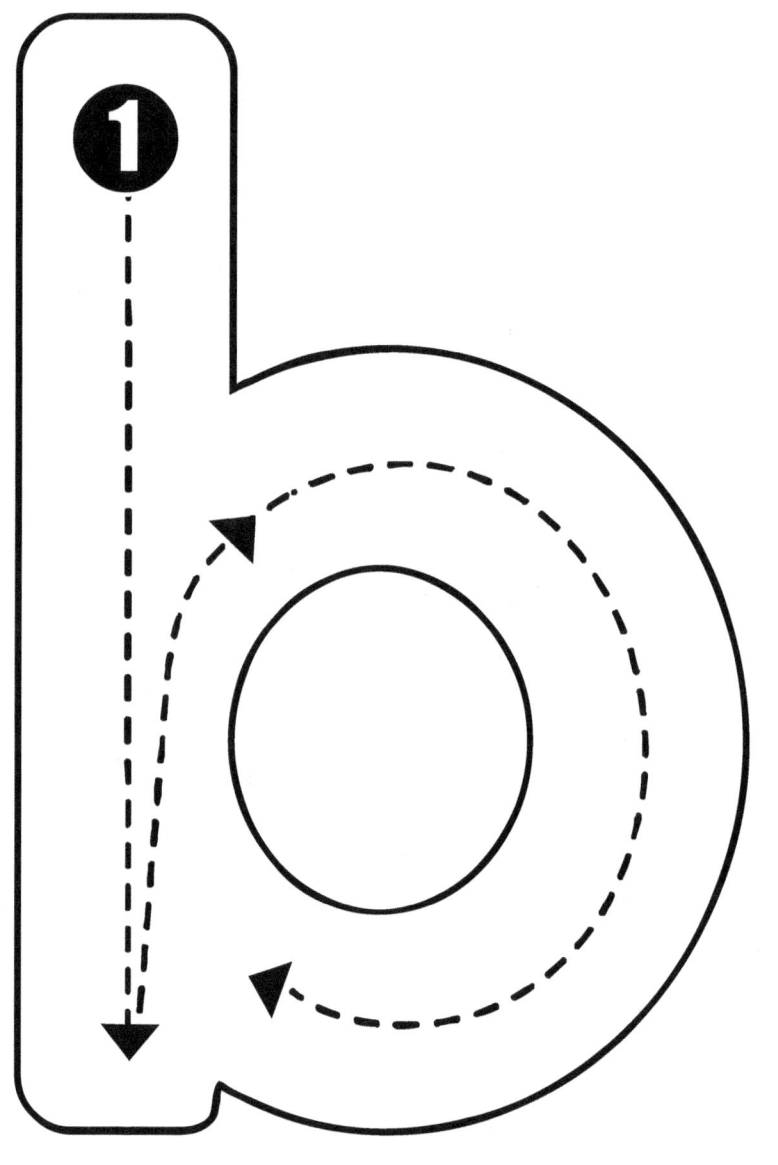

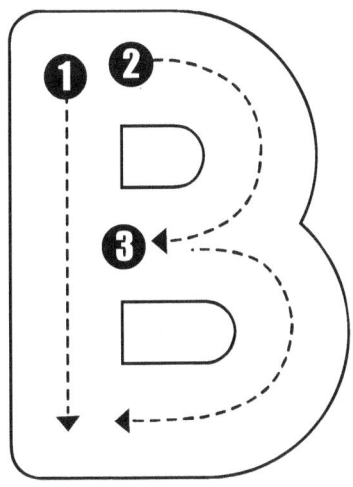 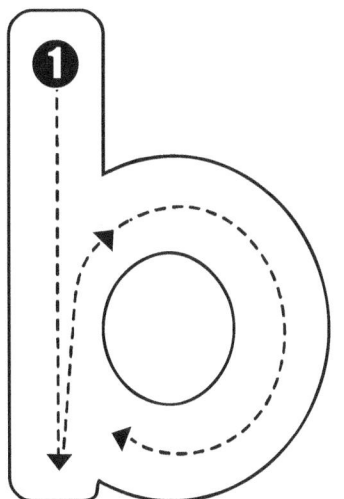

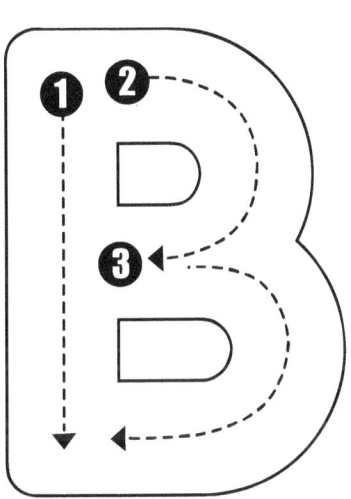 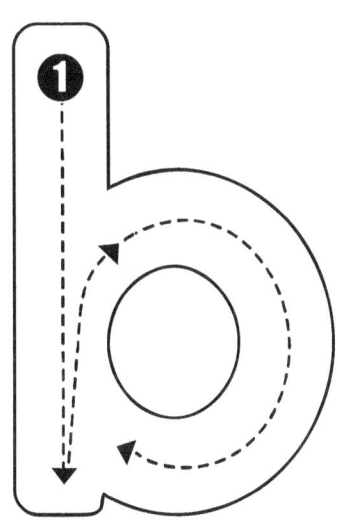

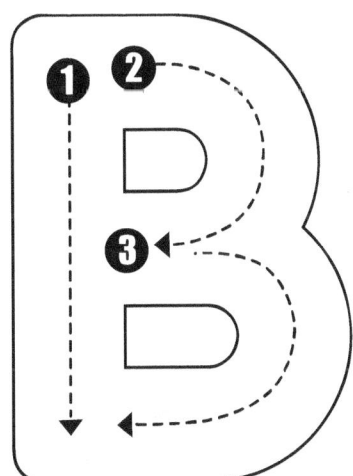 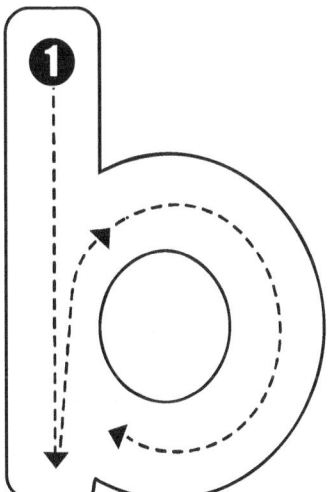

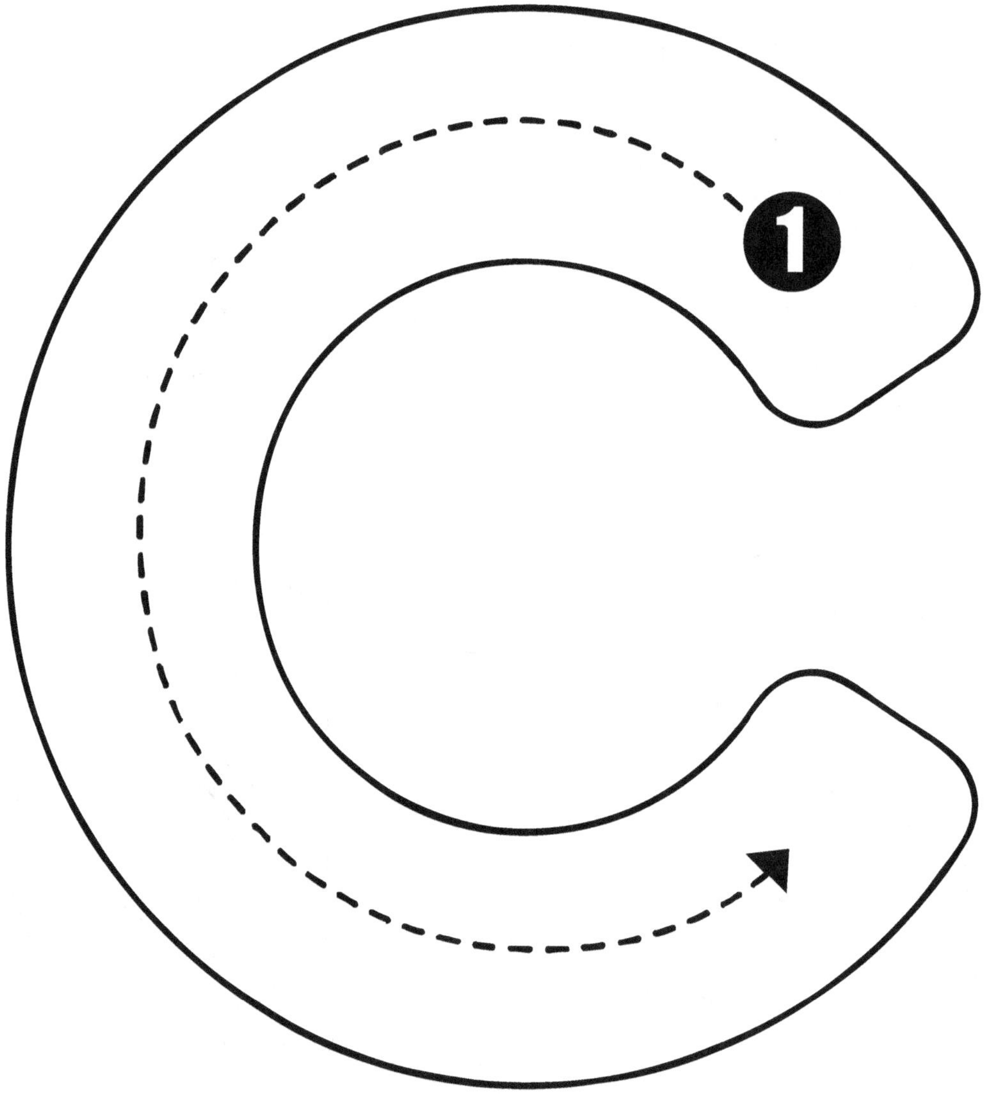

CAT

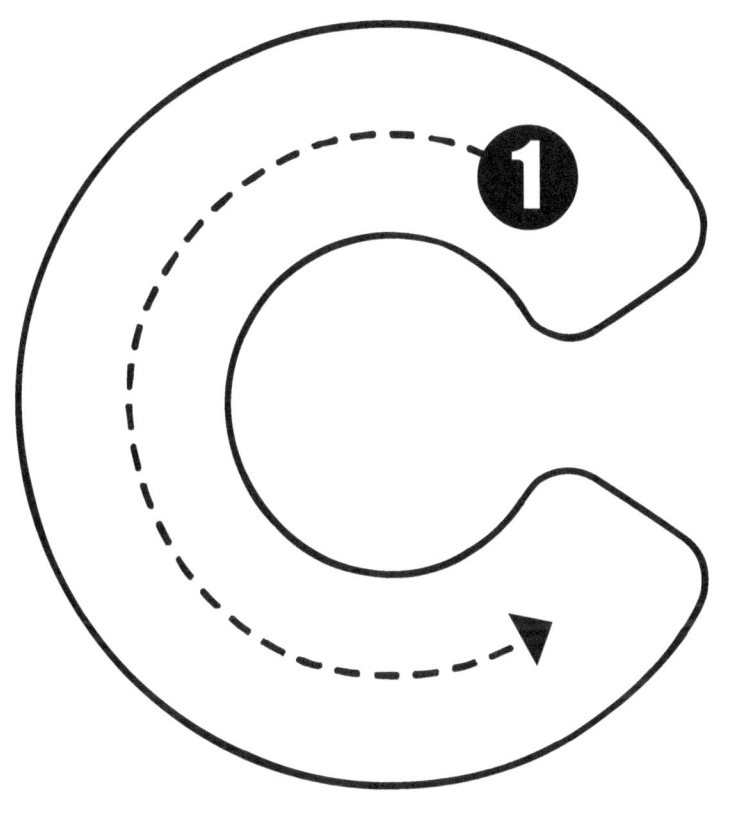

cat

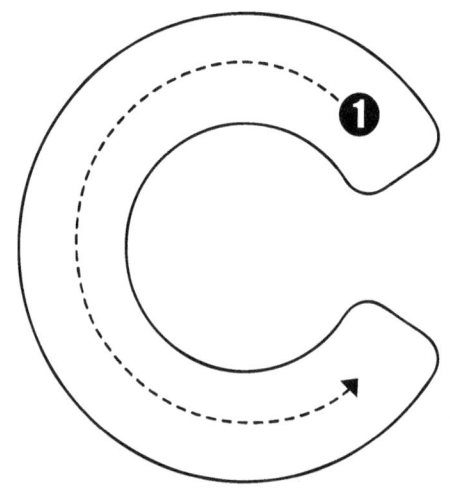 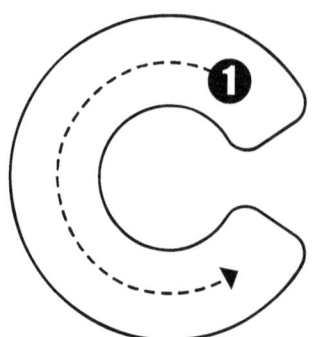

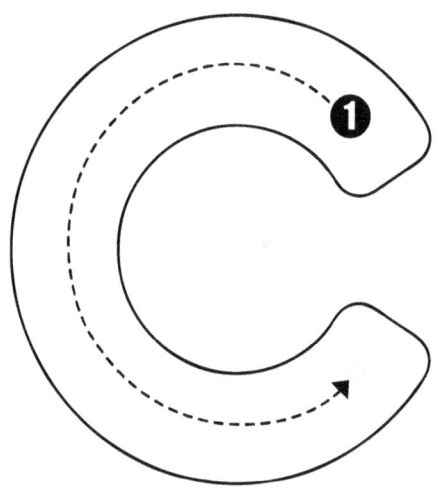 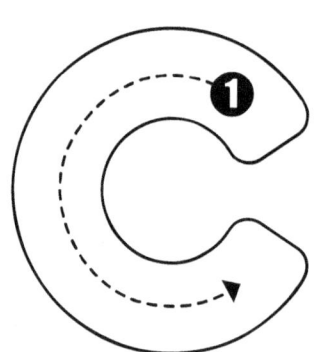

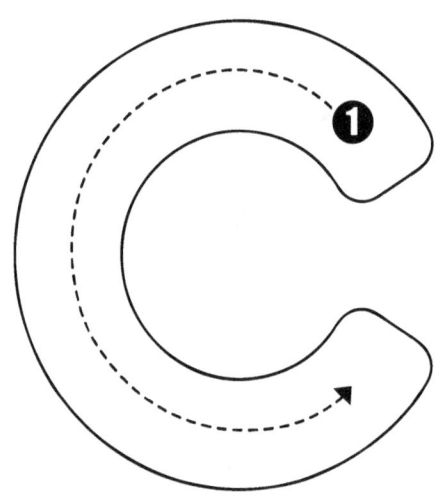 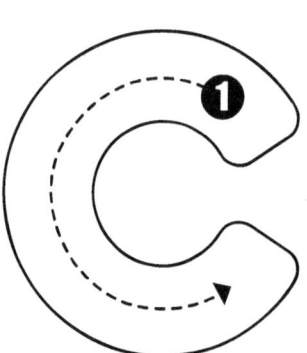

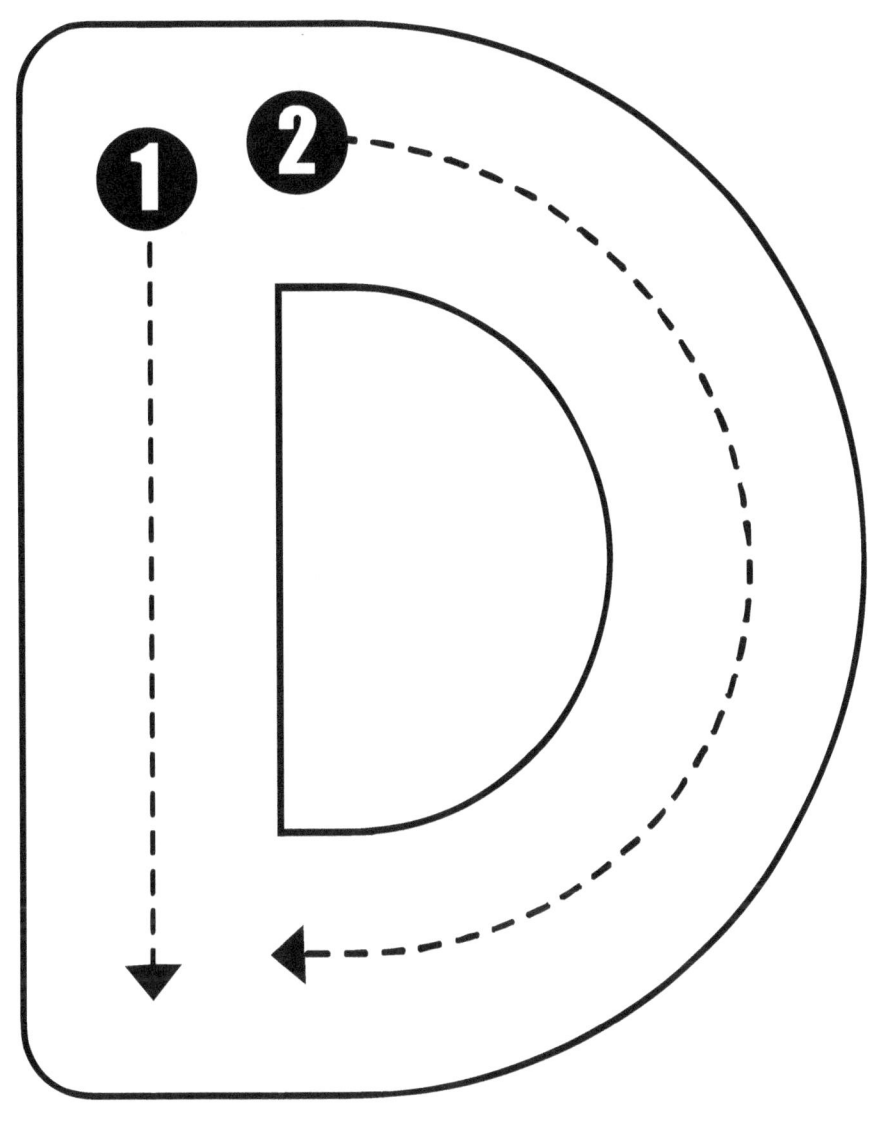

DOG

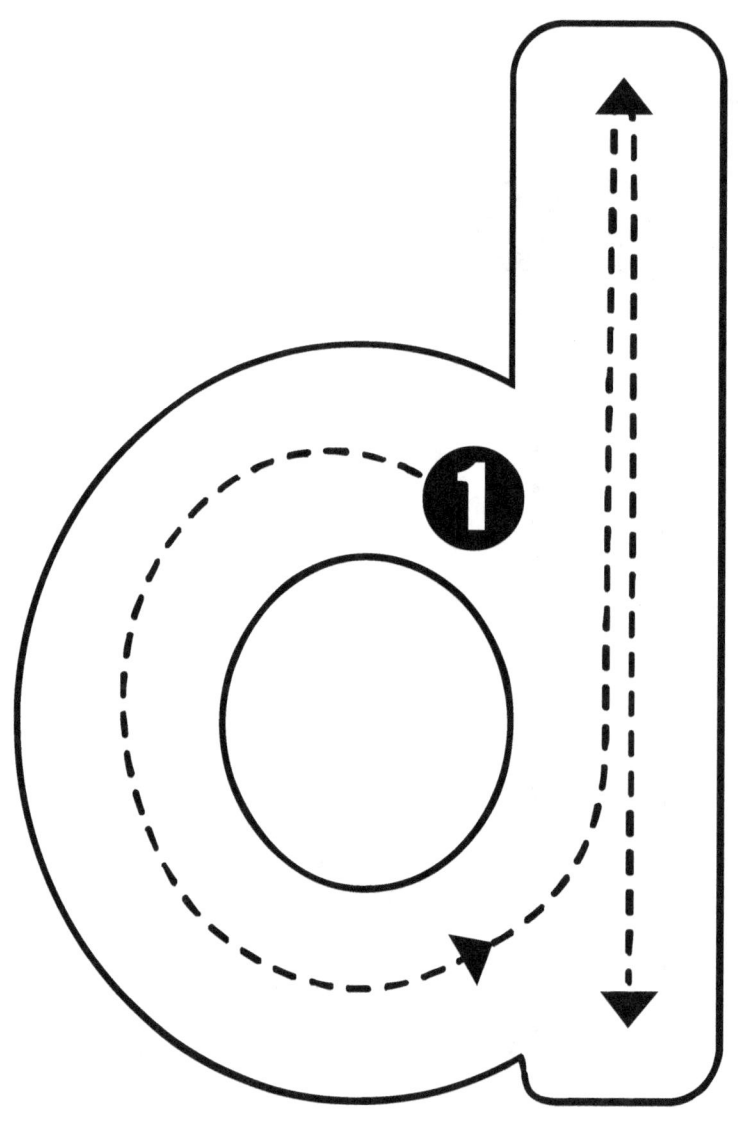

dog

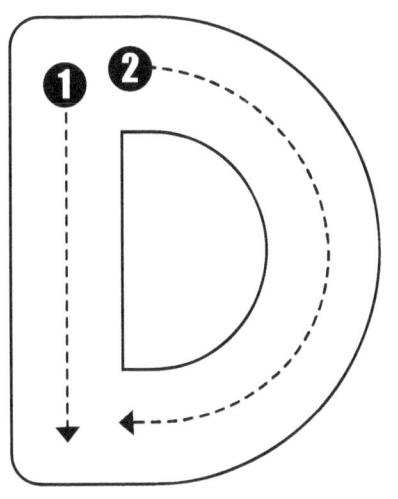 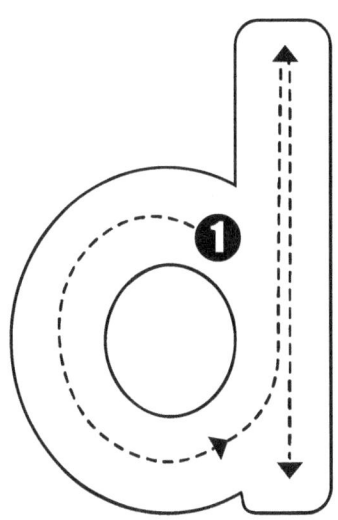

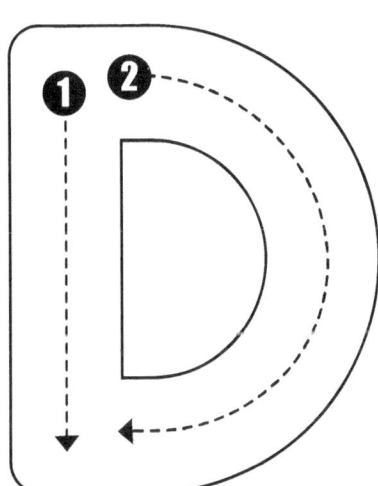 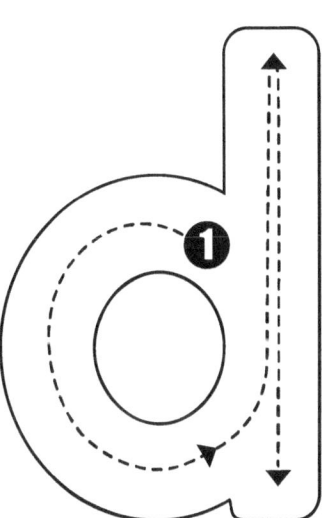

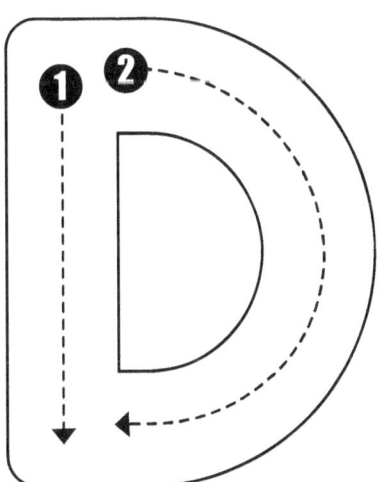 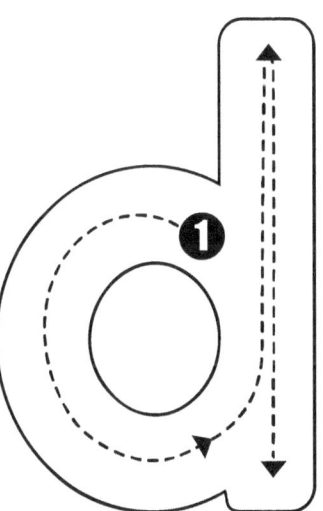

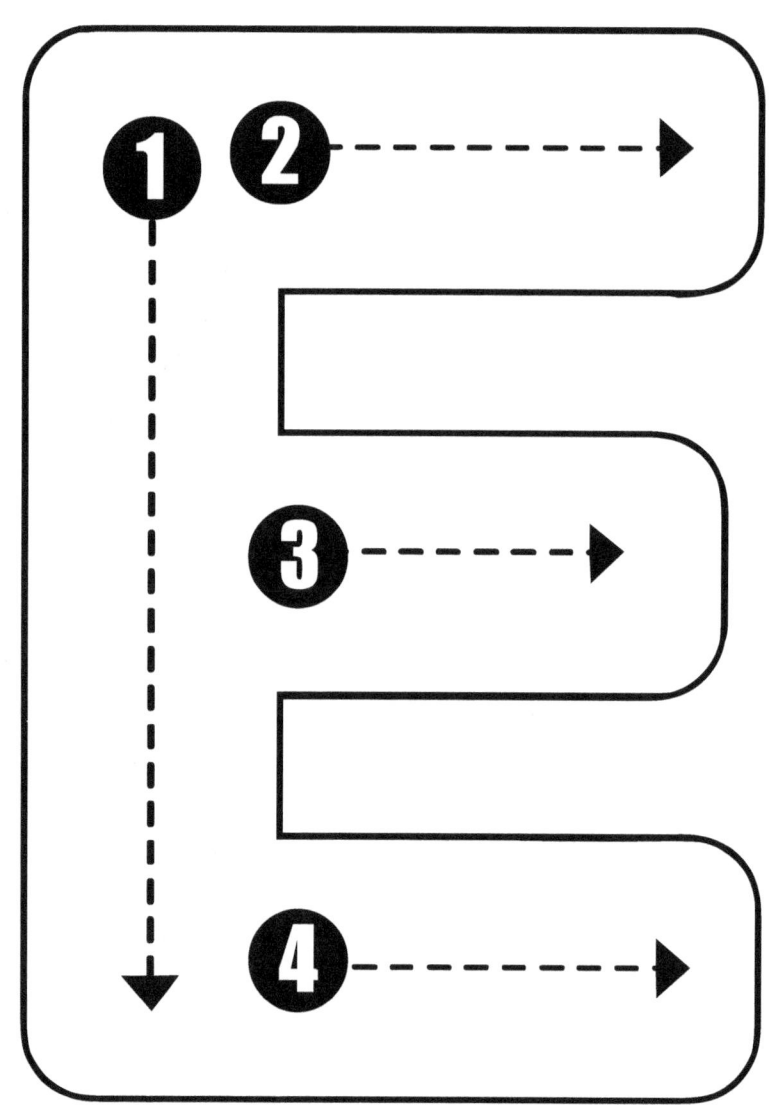

EGG

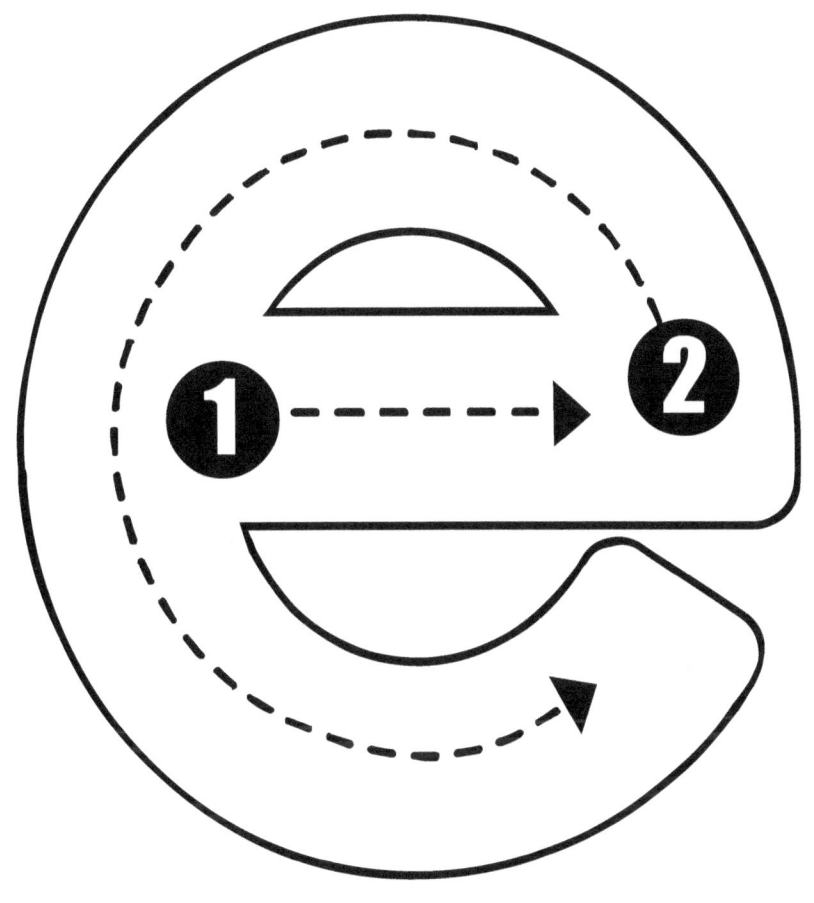

egg

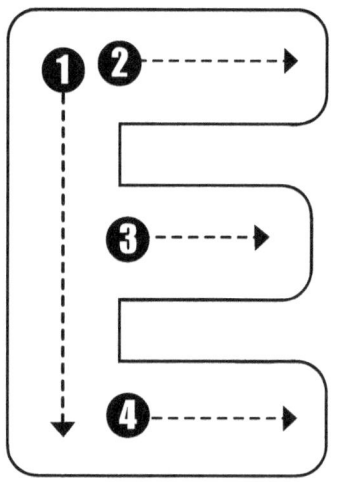 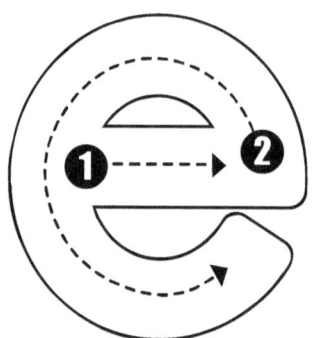

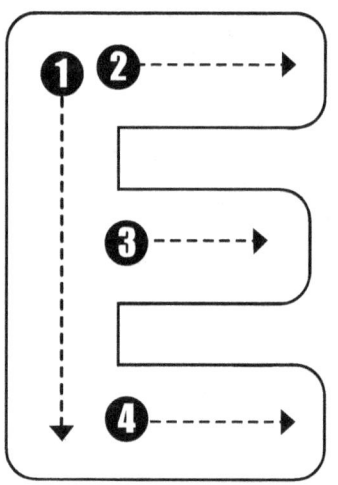 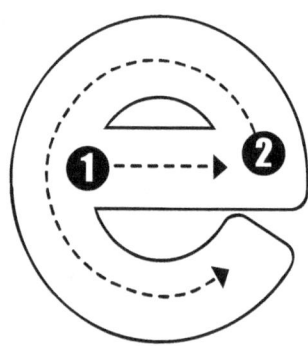

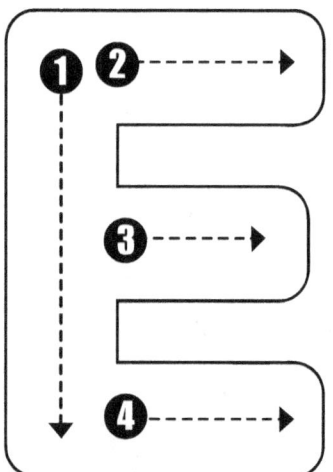 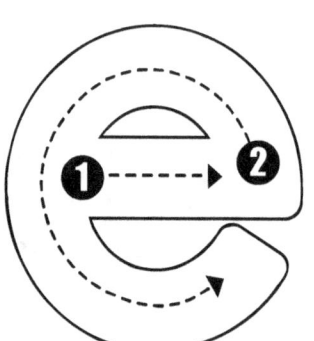

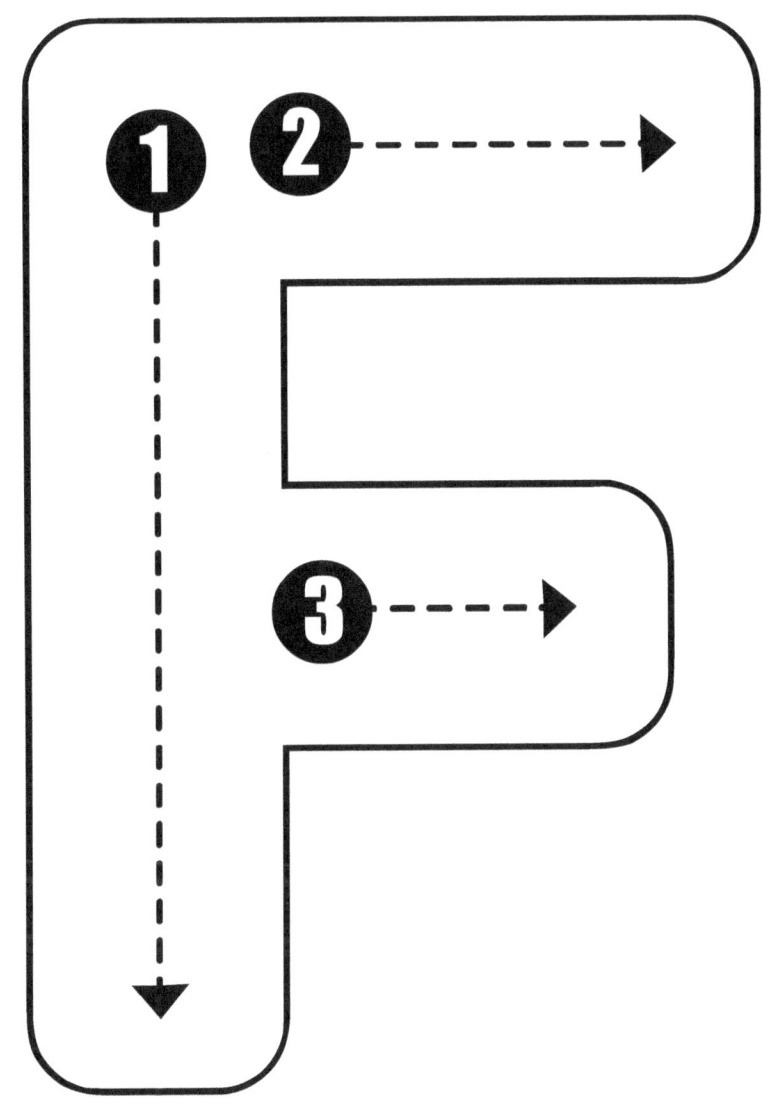

FROG

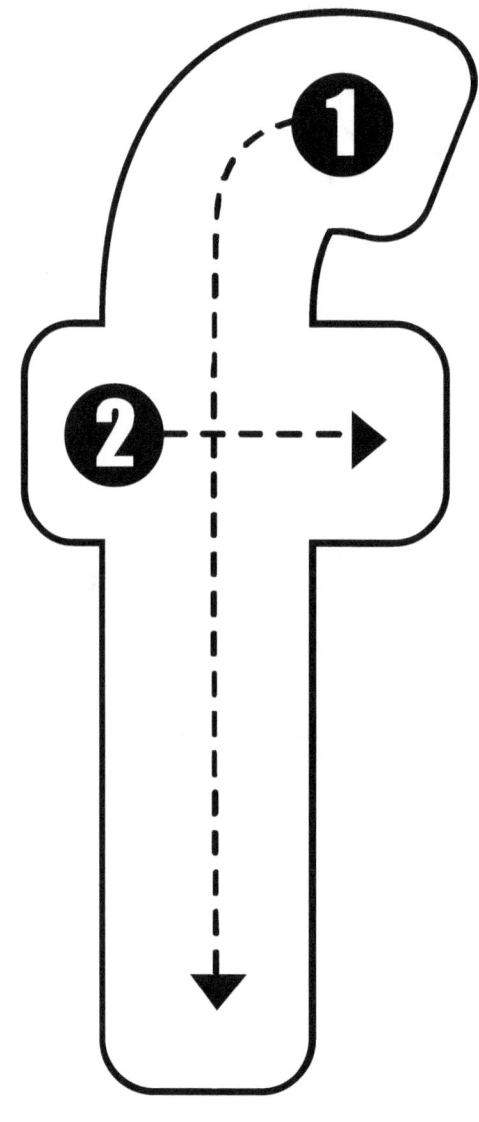

frog

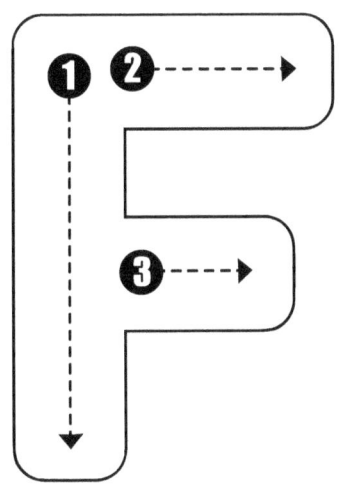 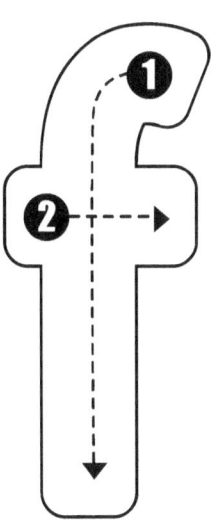

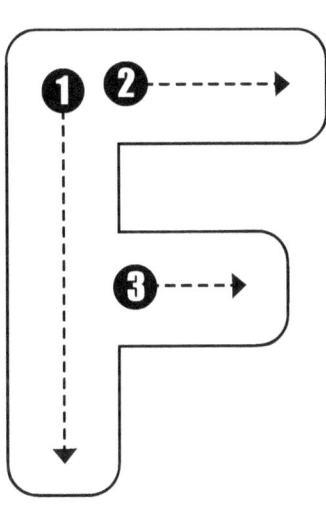 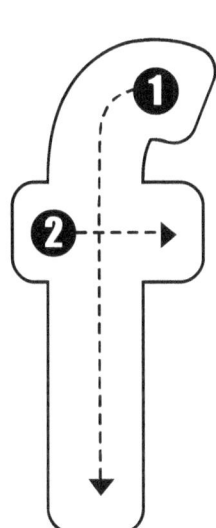

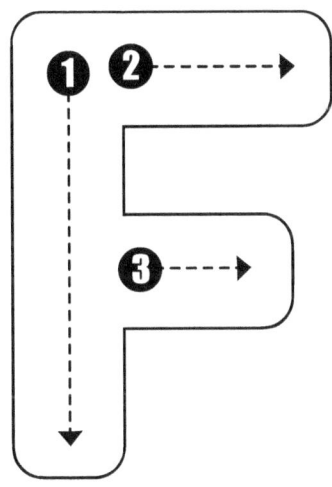 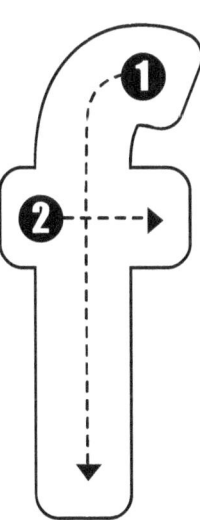

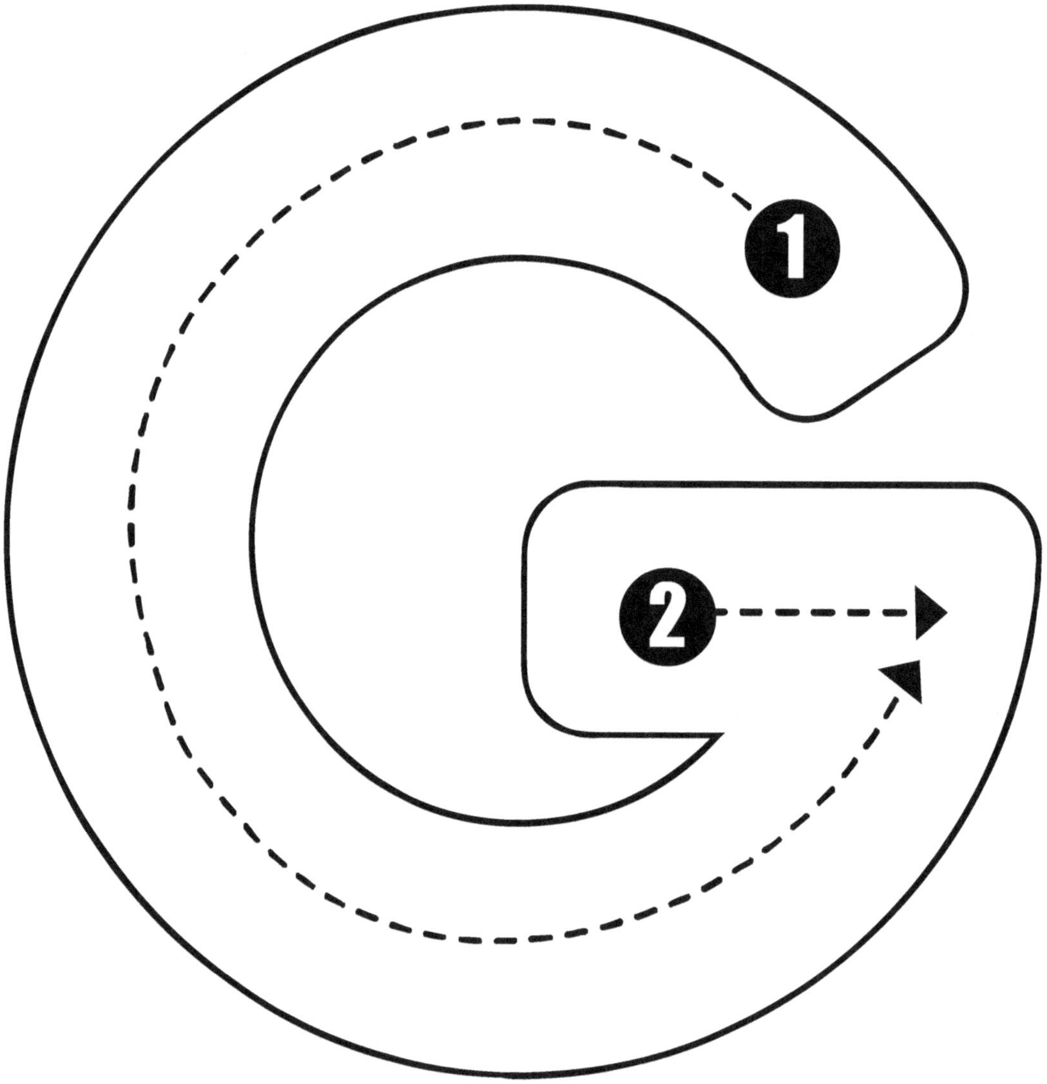

GOAT

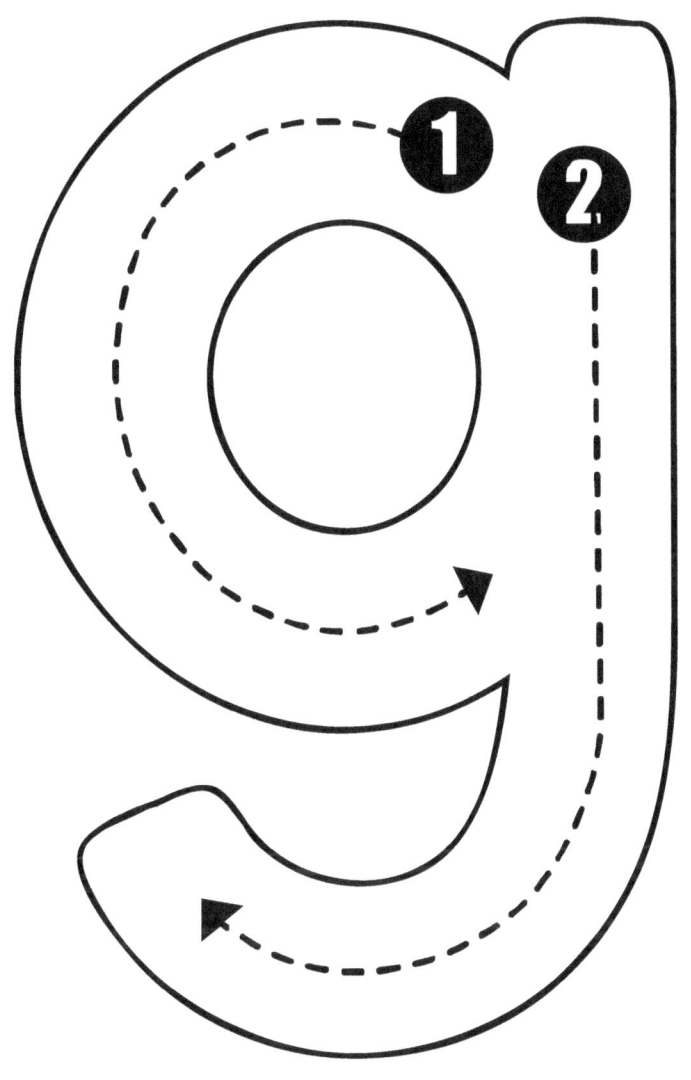

goat

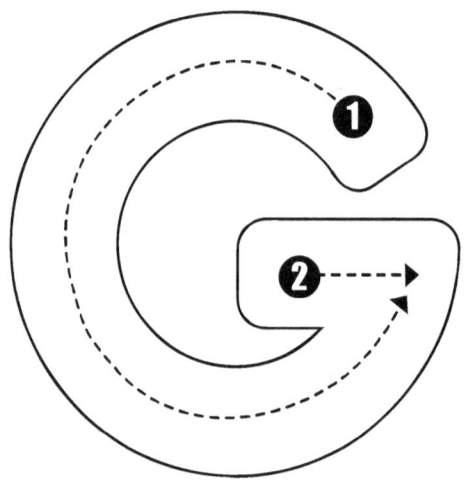 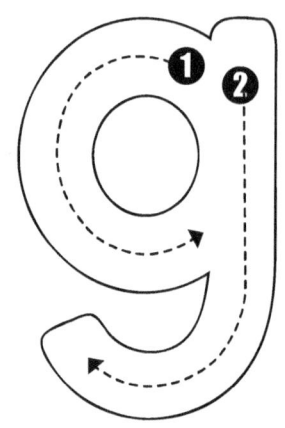

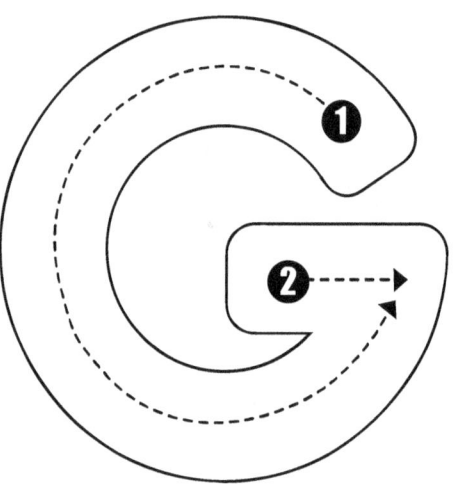 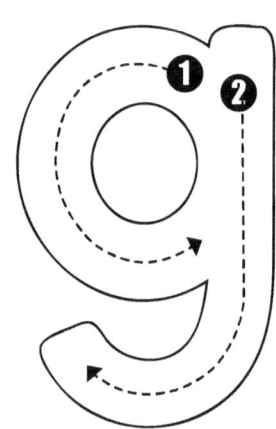

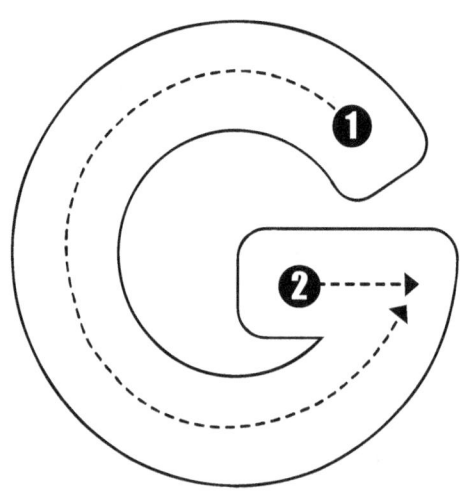 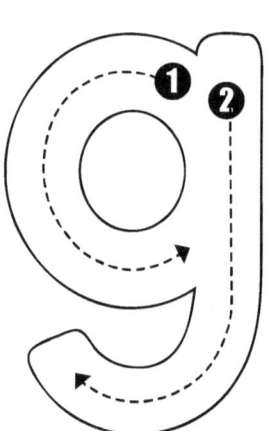

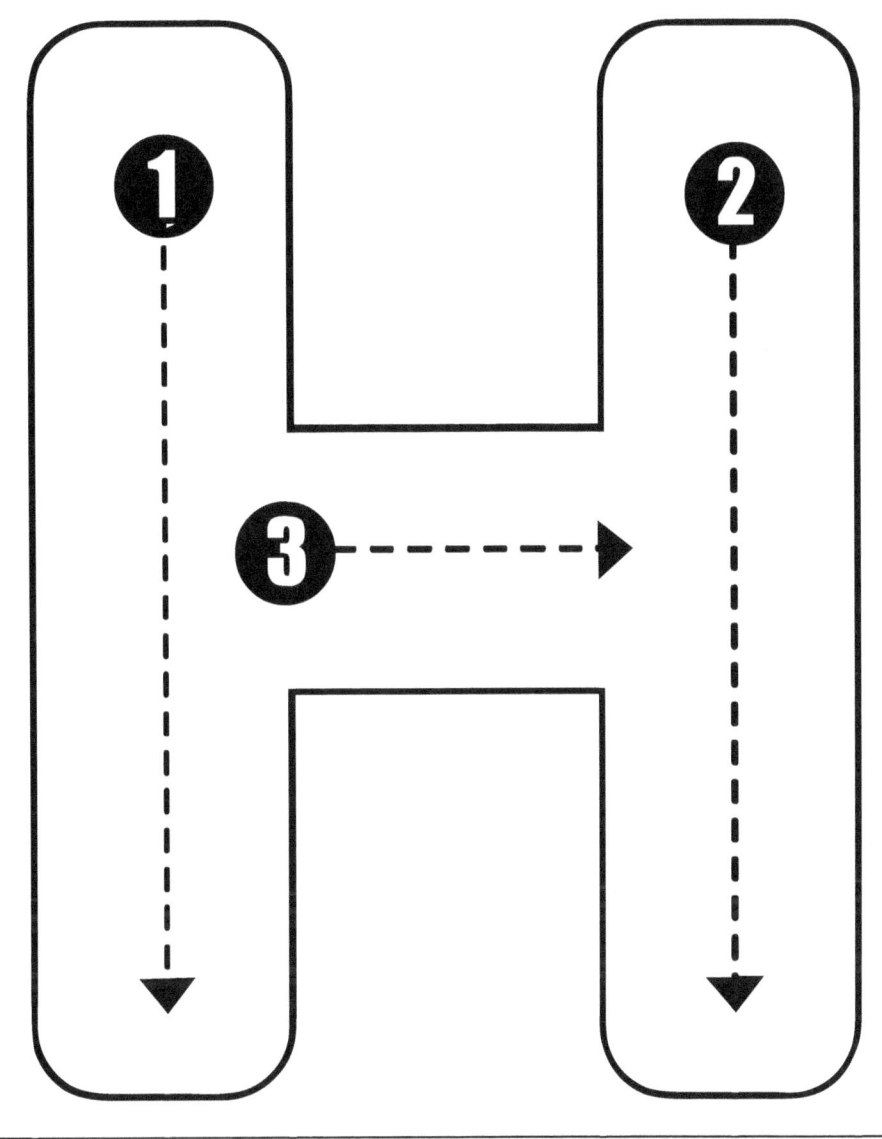

HAT

hat

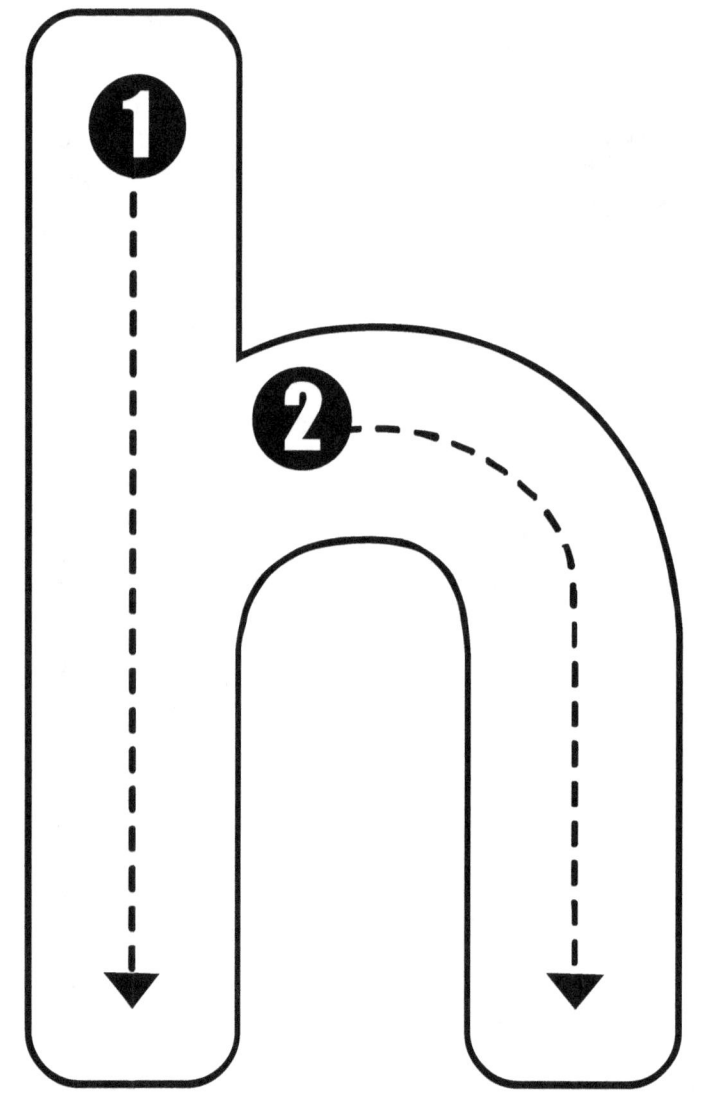

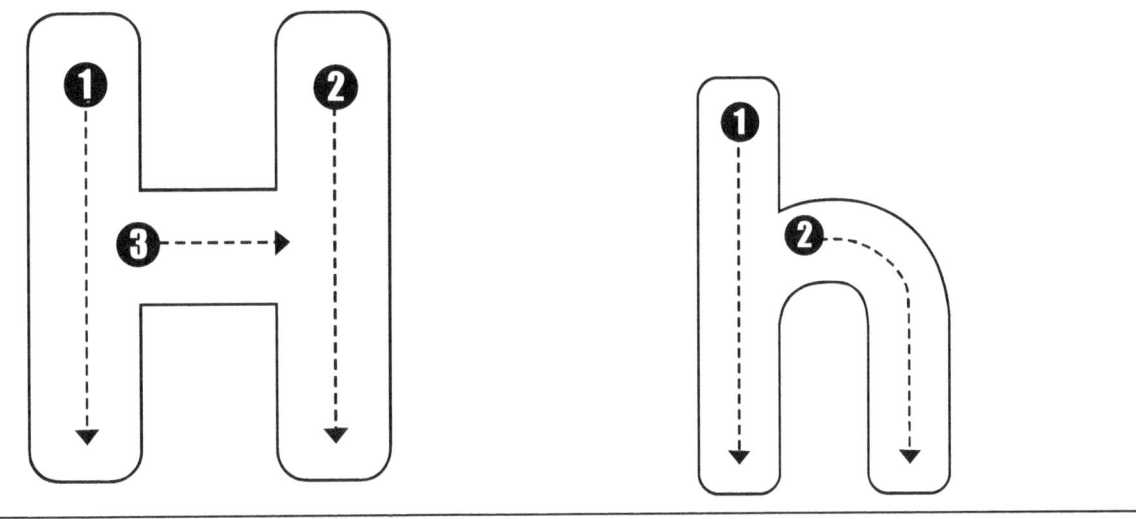
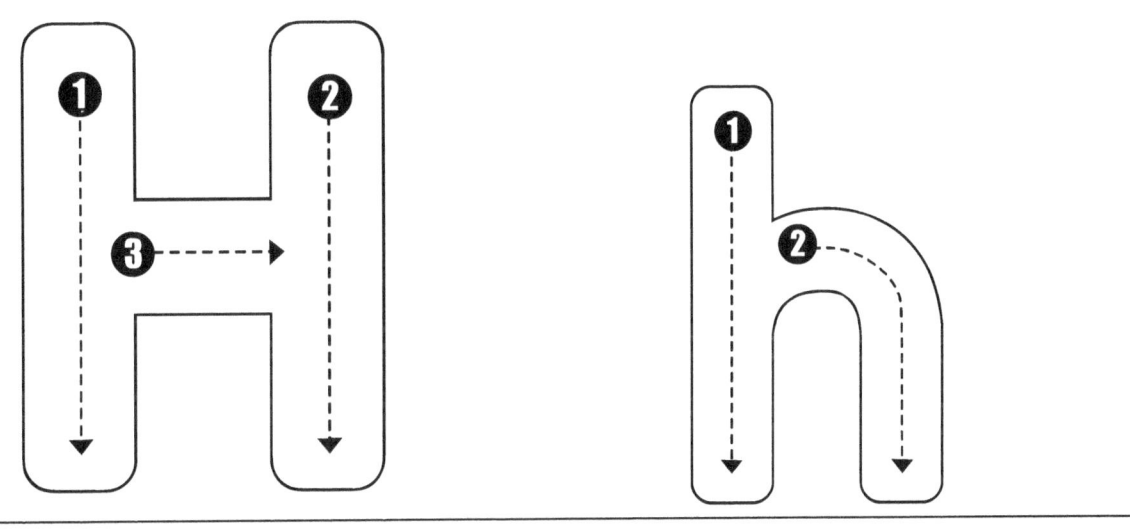
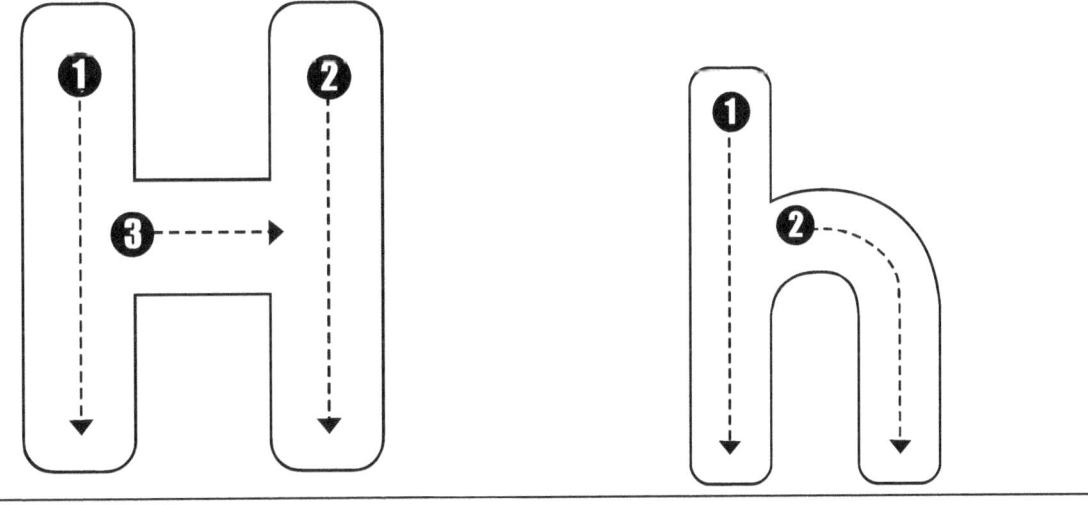

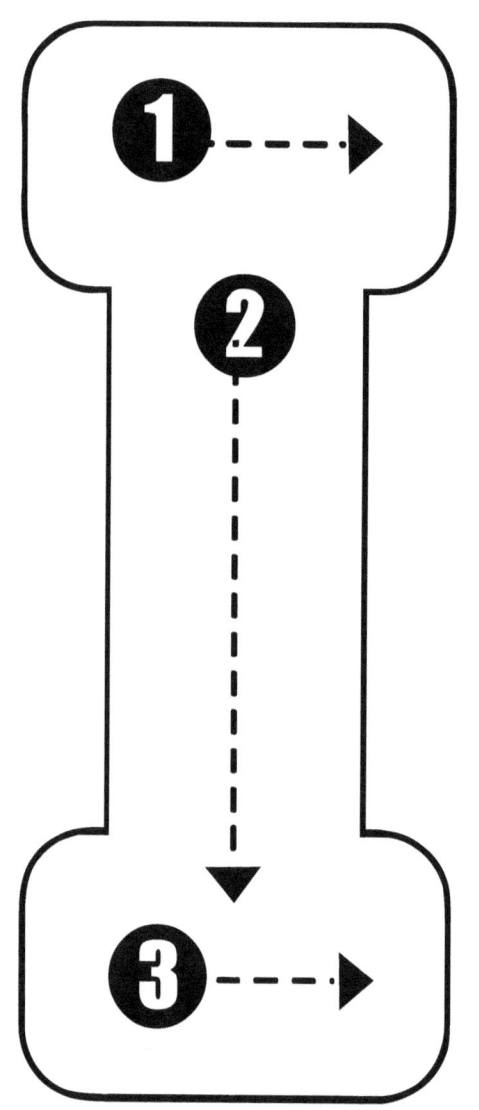

ICE

ice

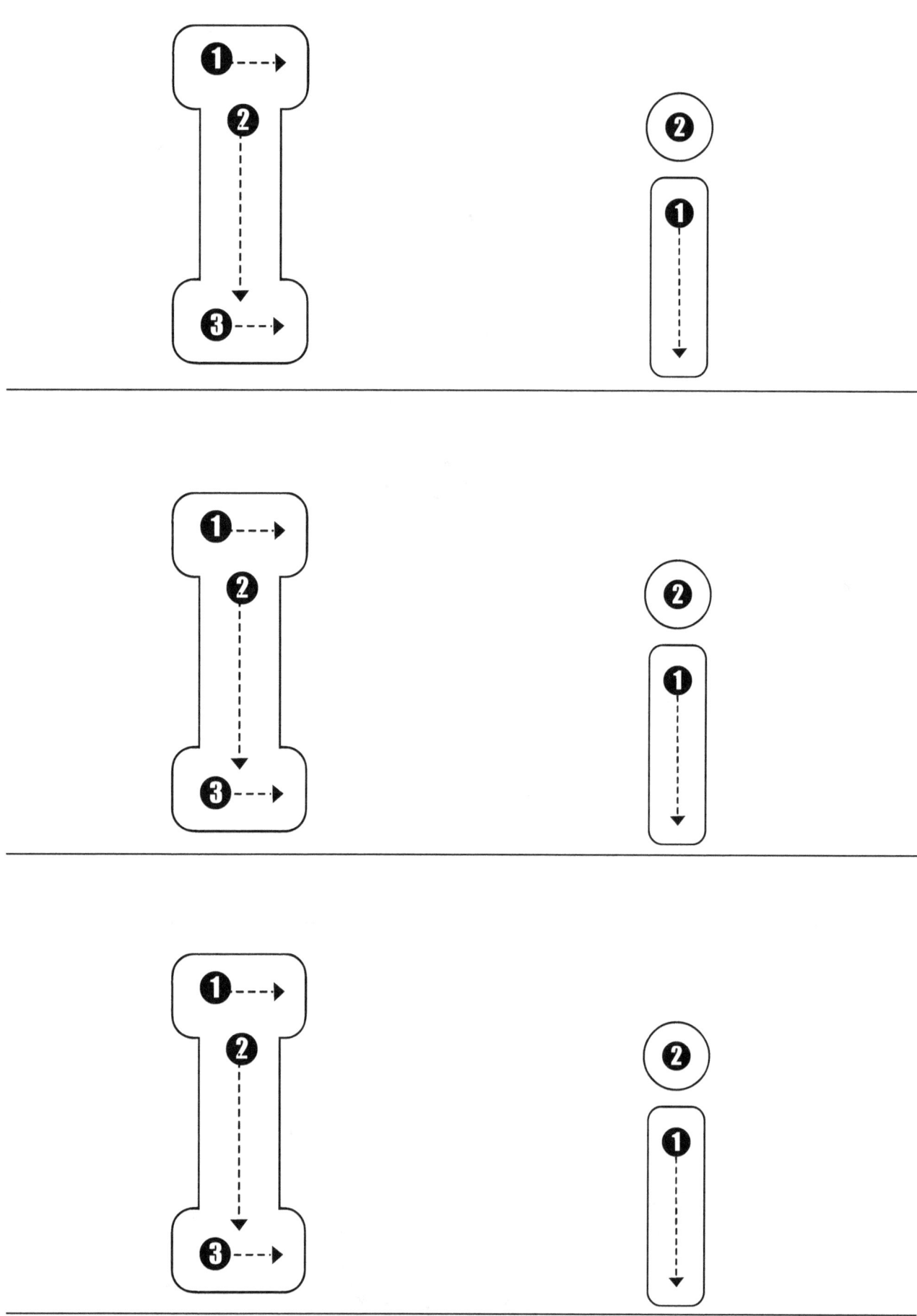

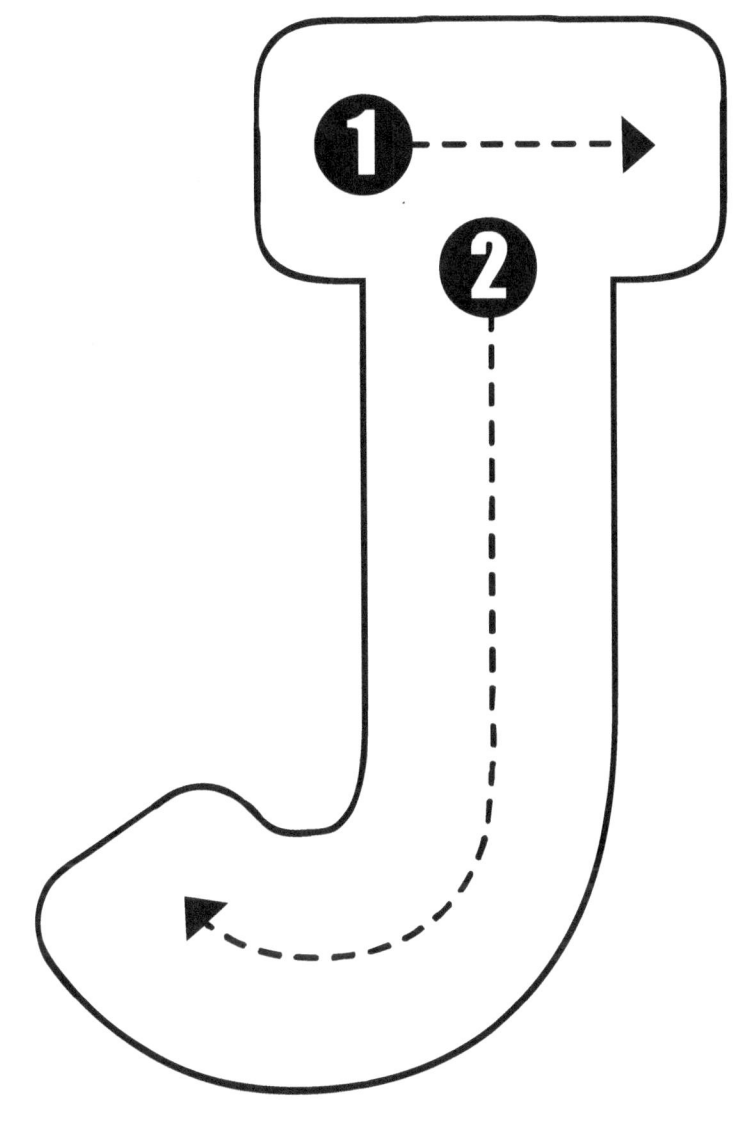

JAR

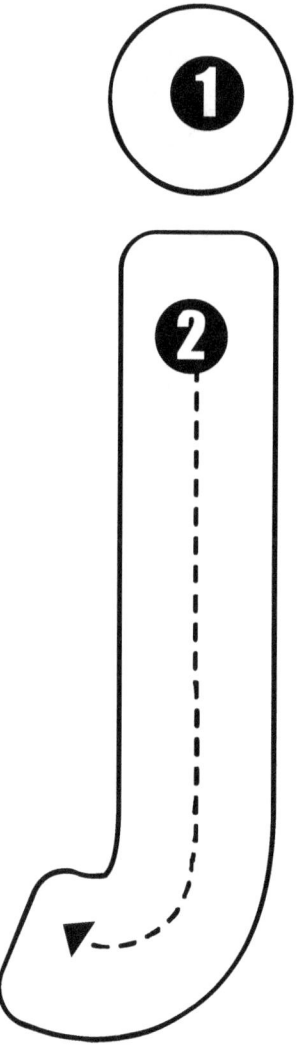

jar

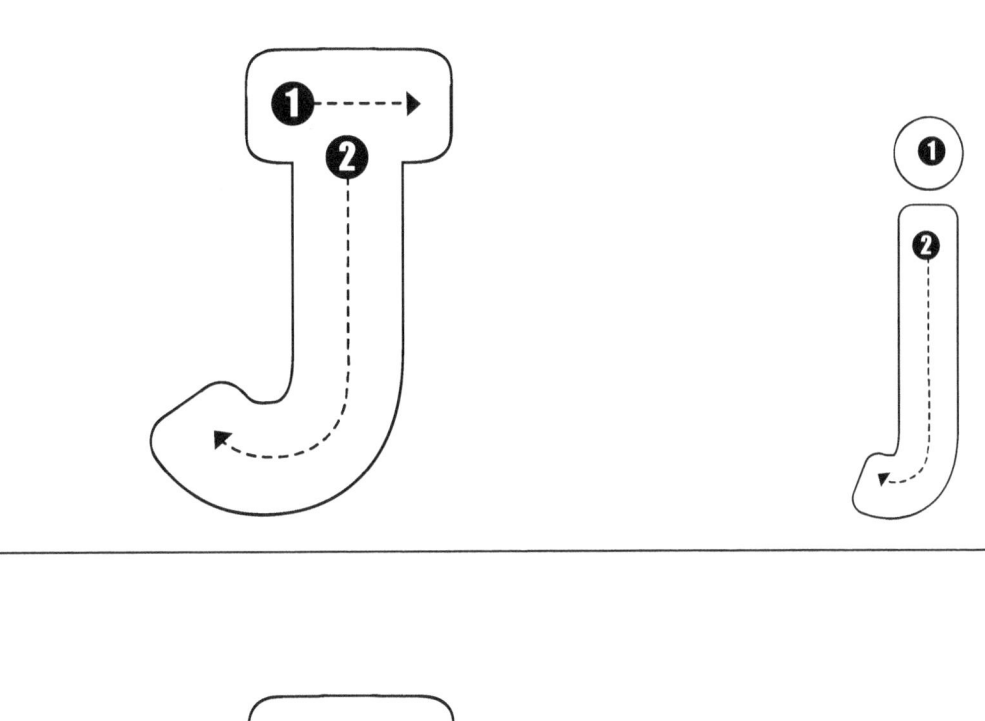
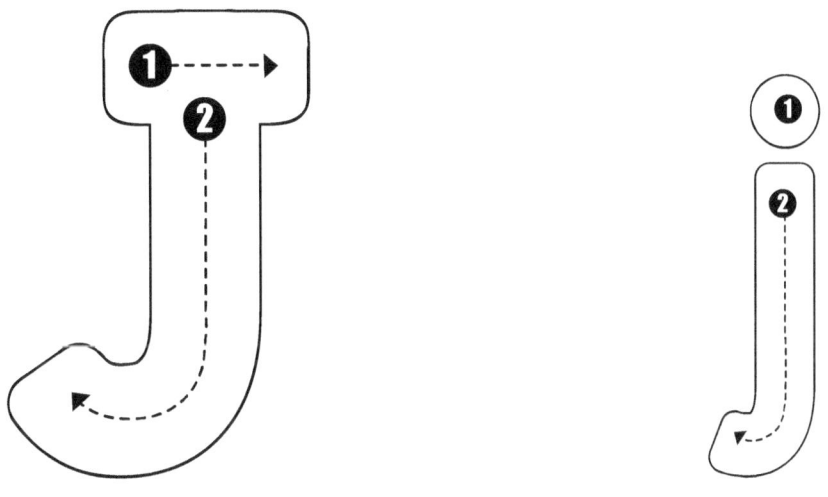
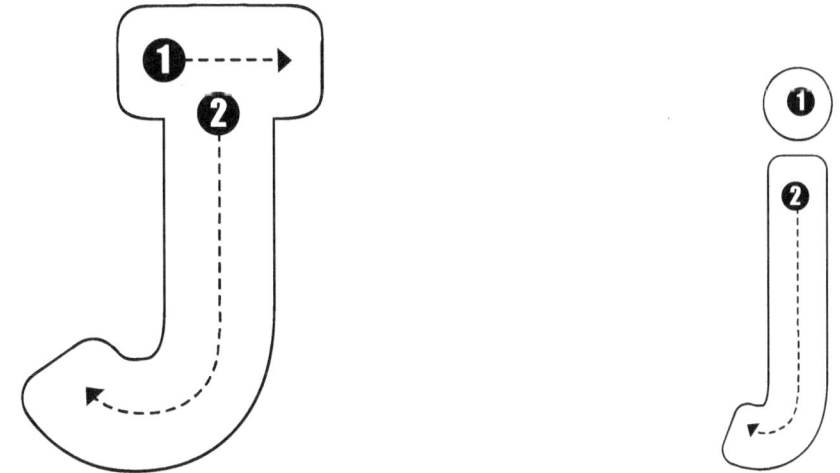

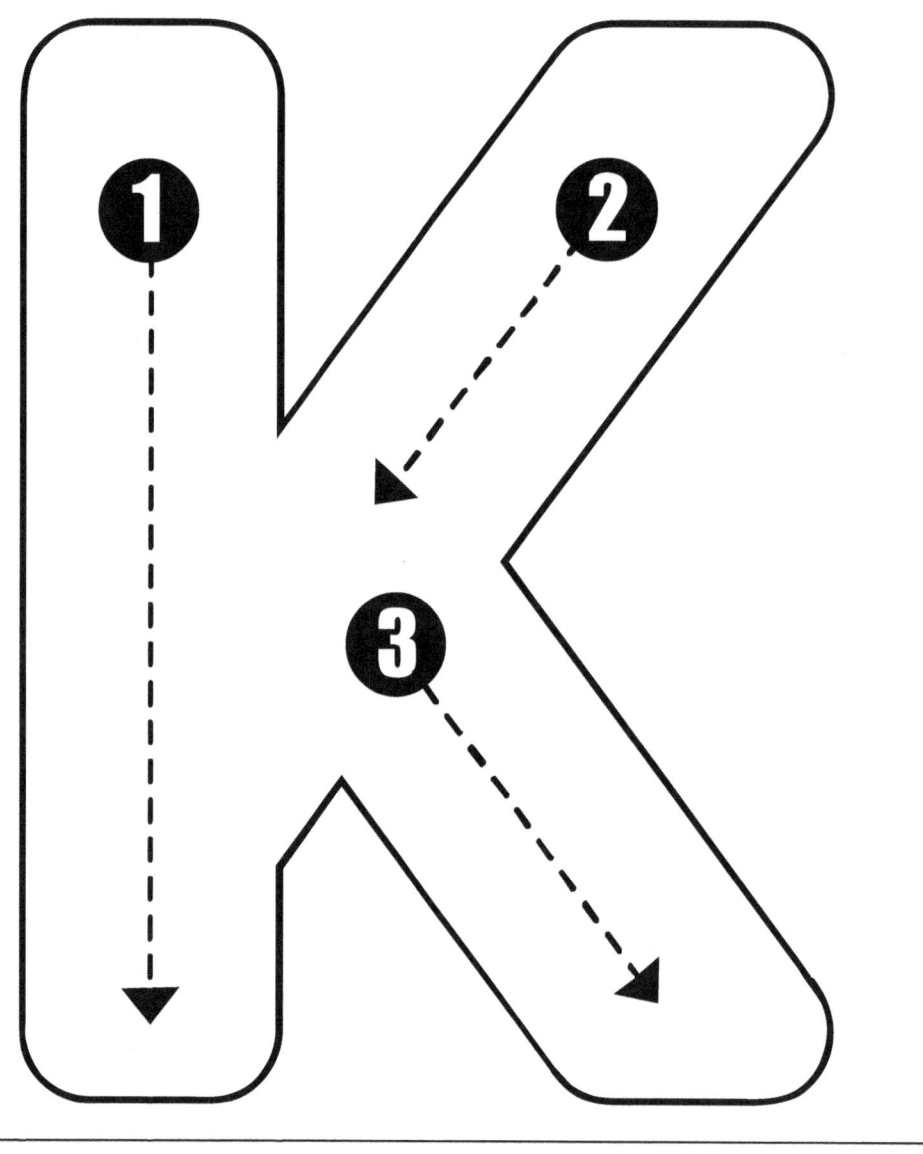

KOALA

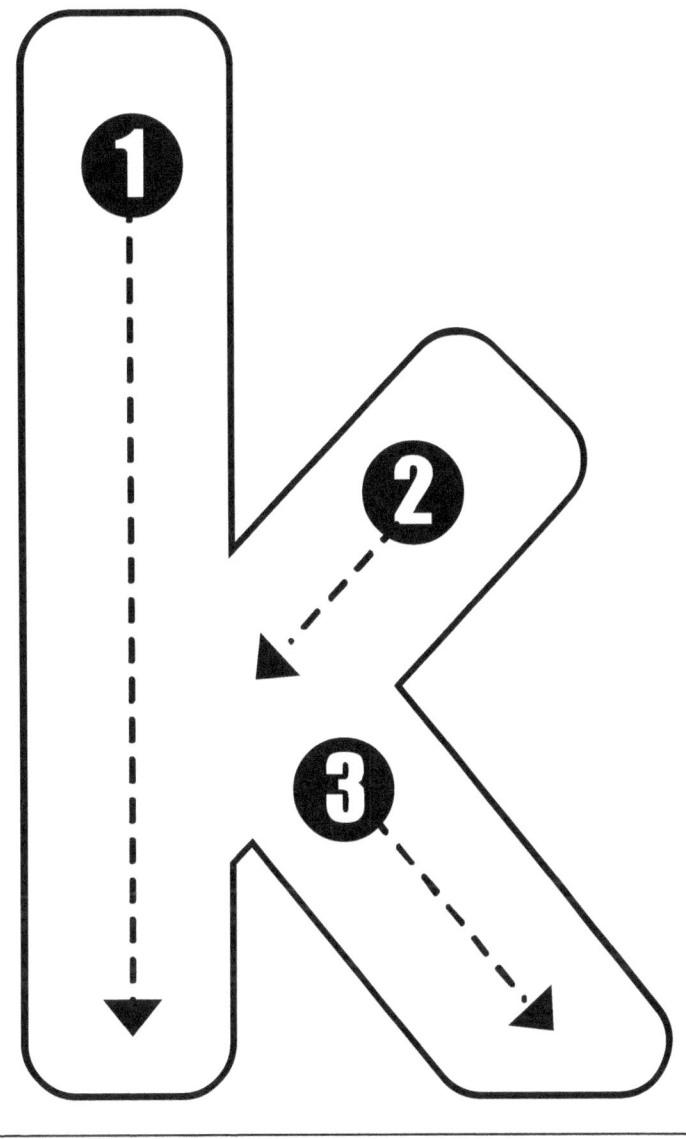

koala

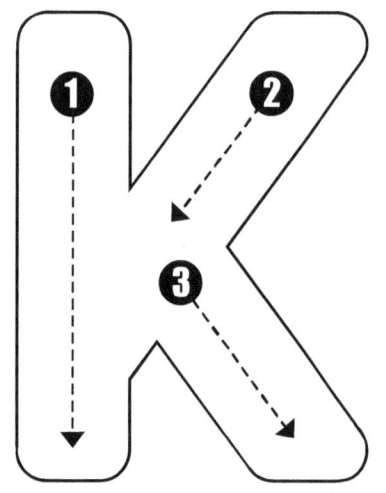 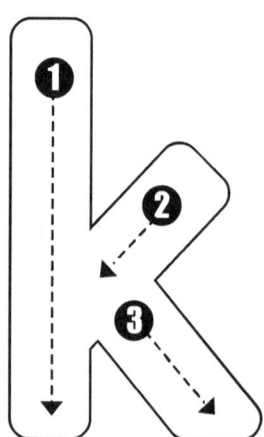

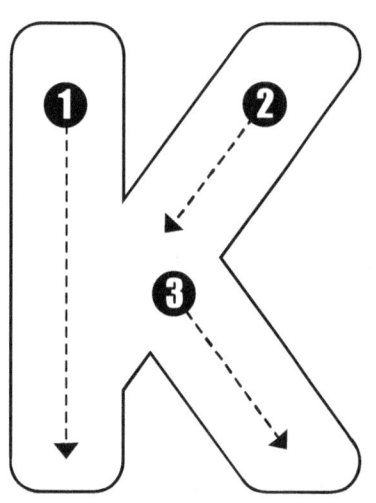 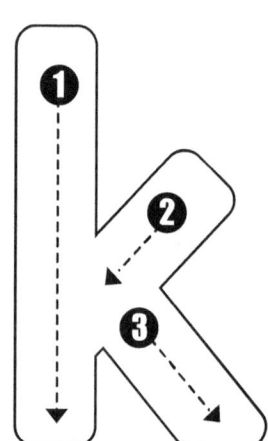

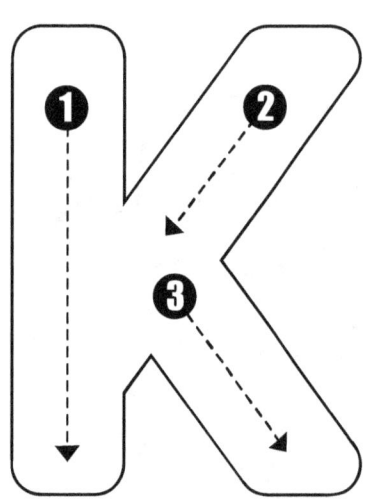 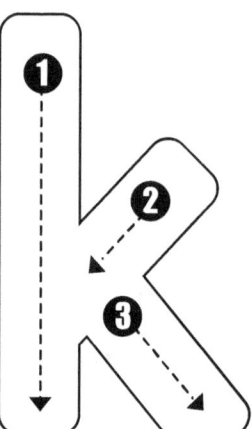

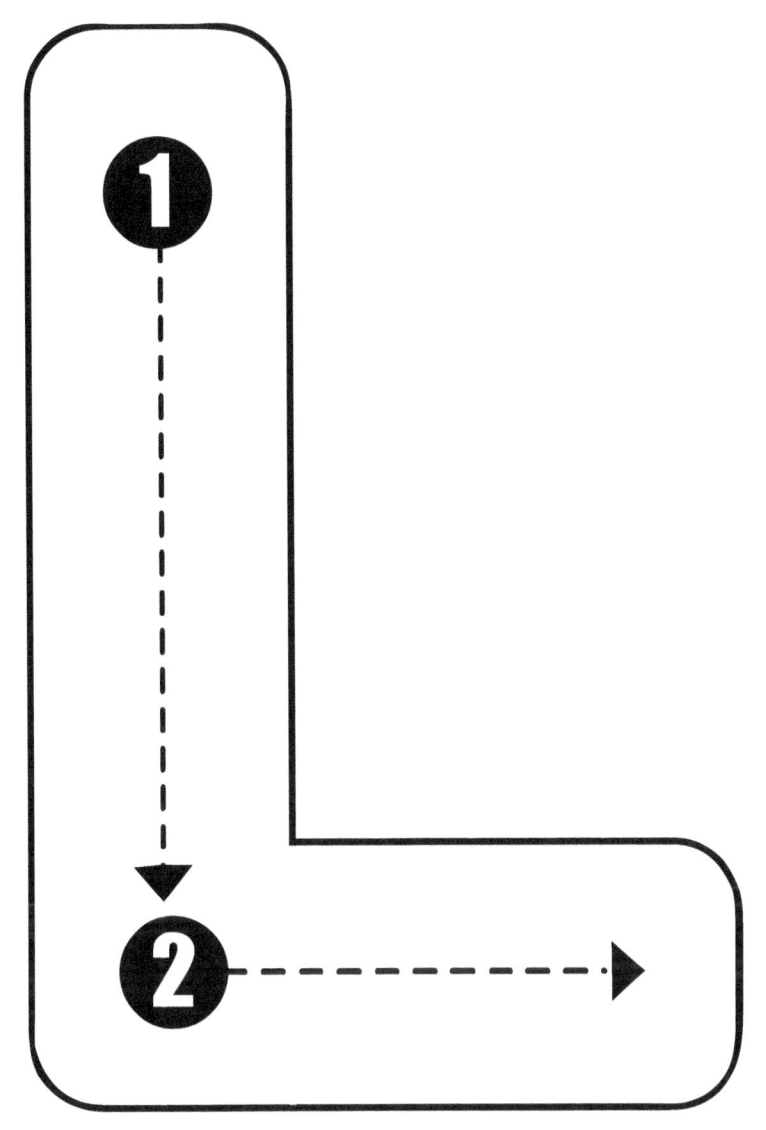

LION

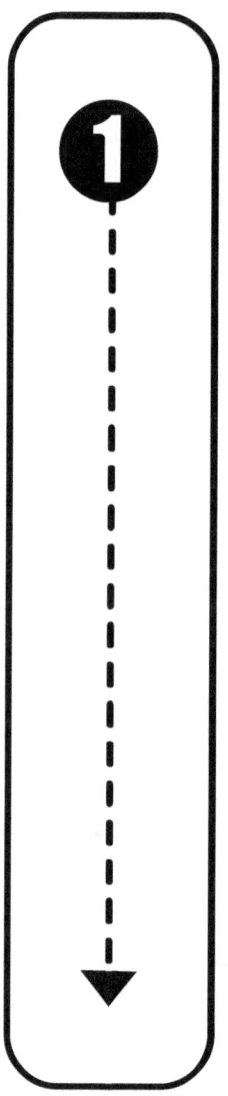

lion

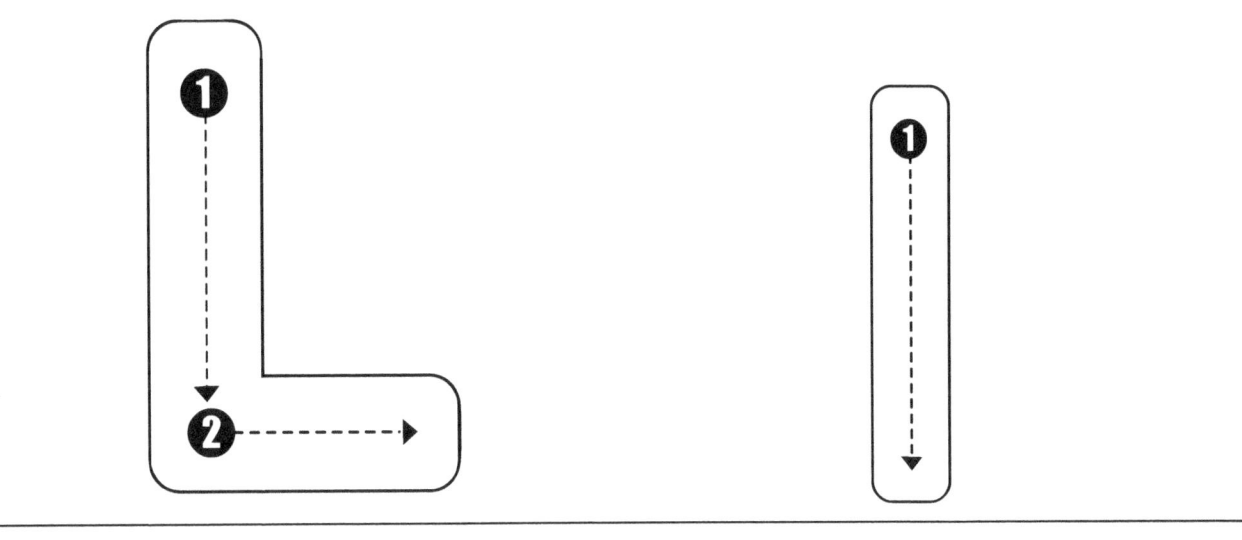
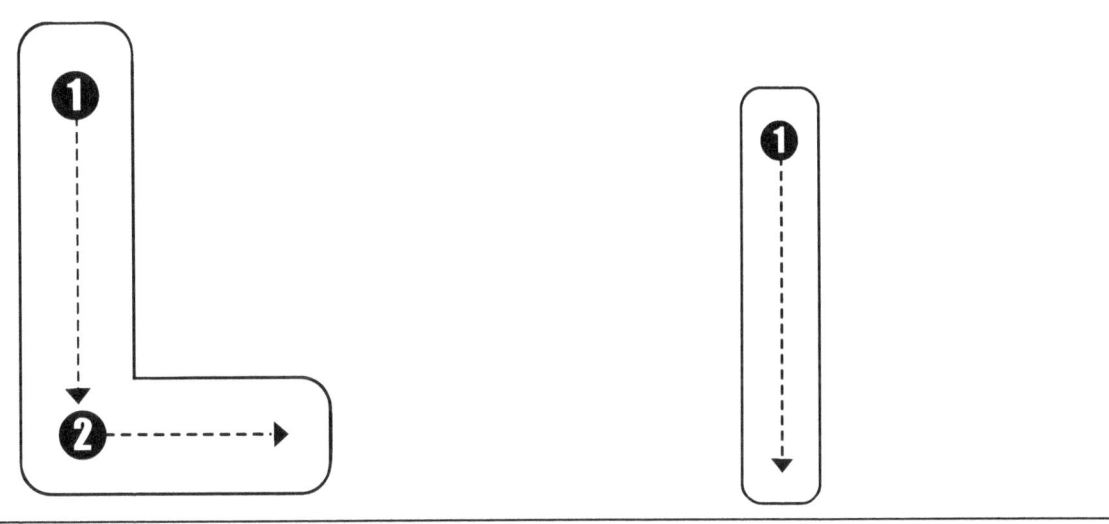

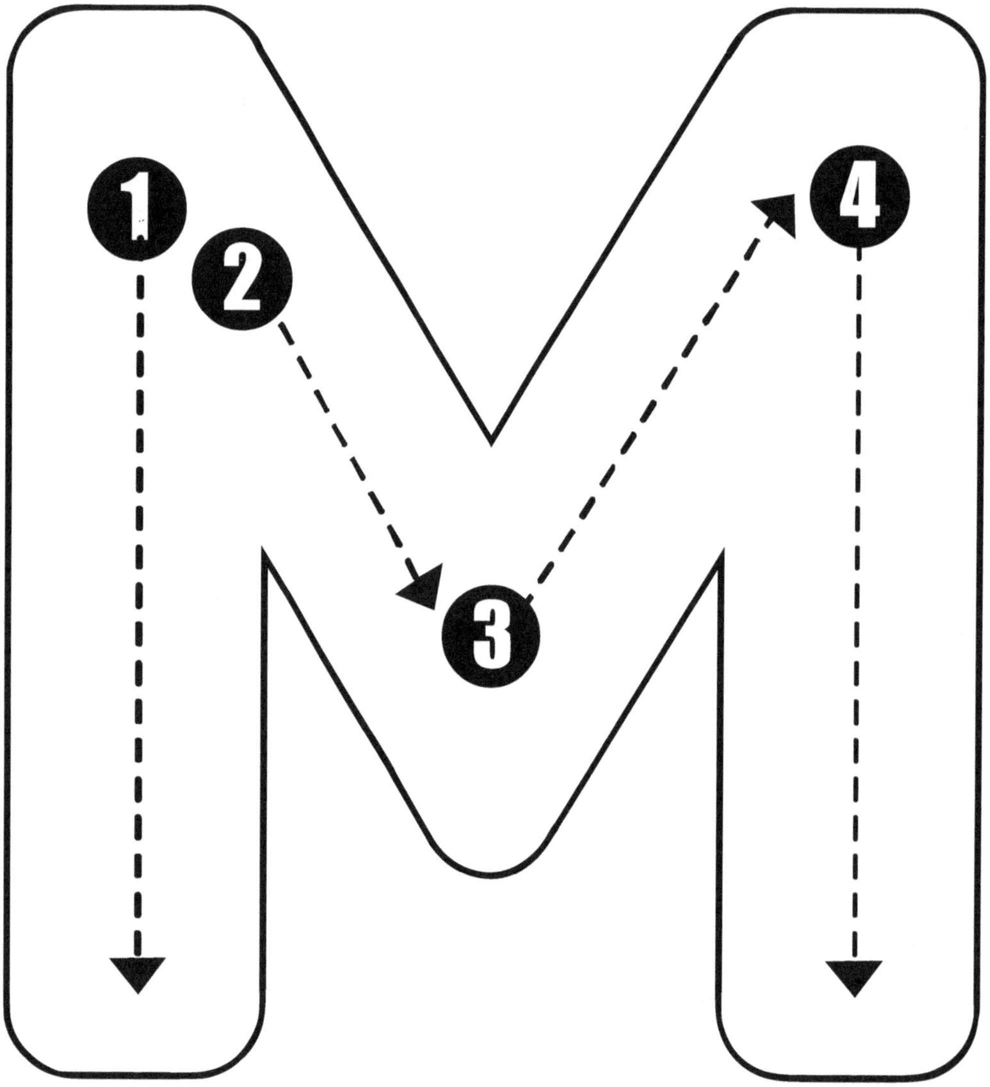

M

MOUSE

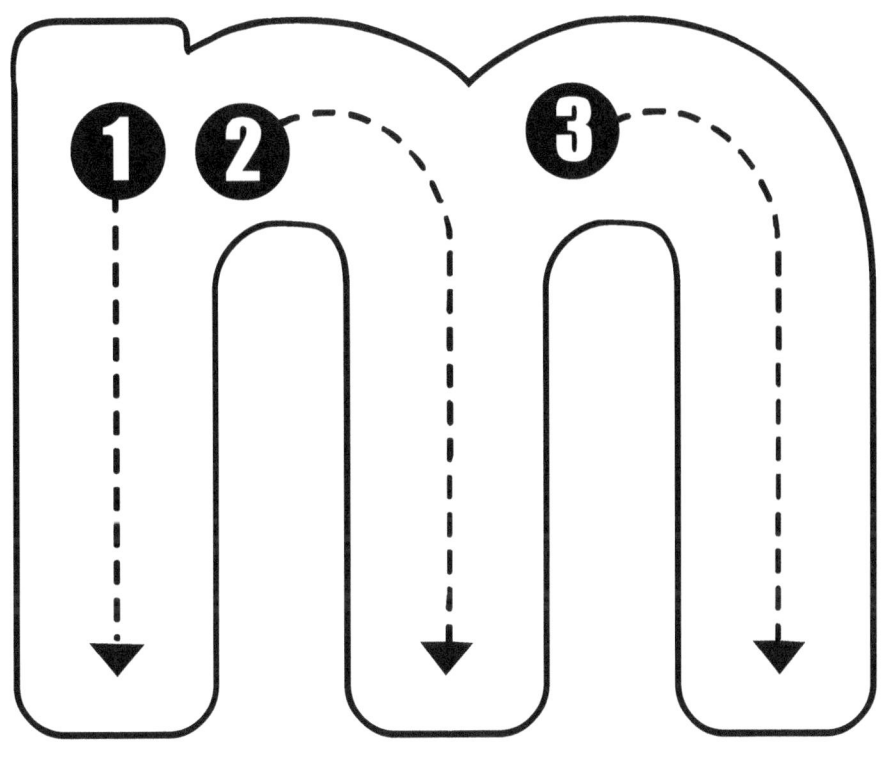

mouse

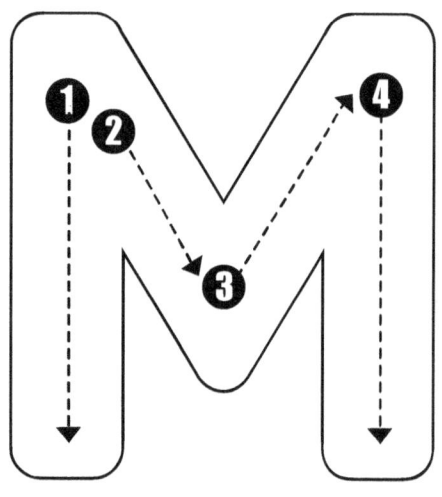 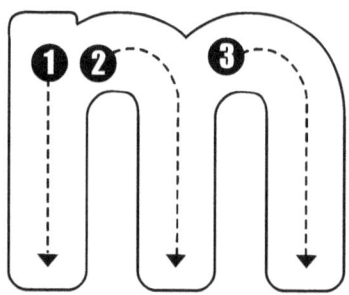

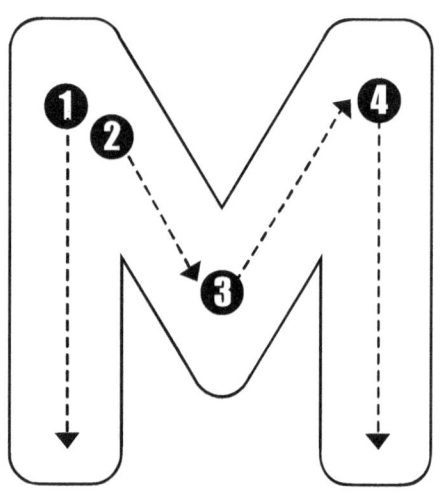 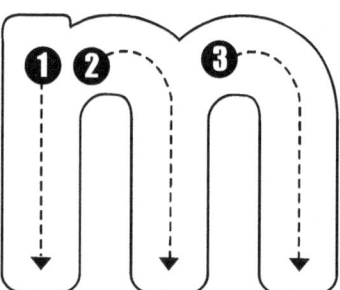

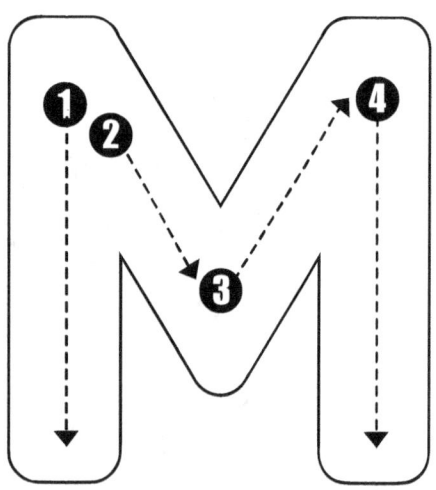 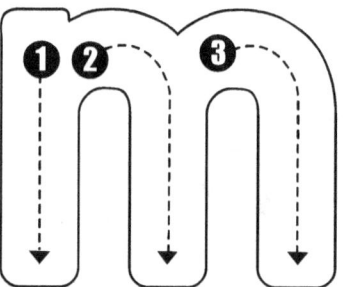

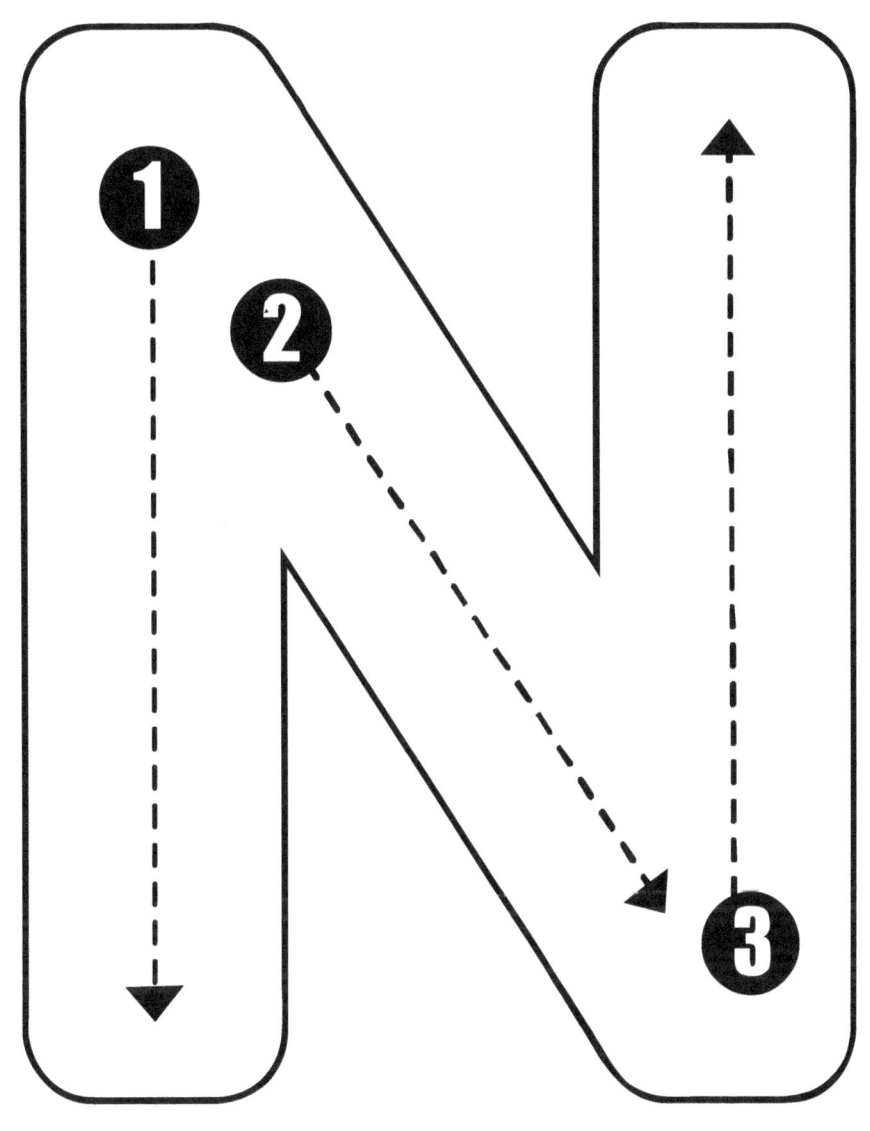

NEST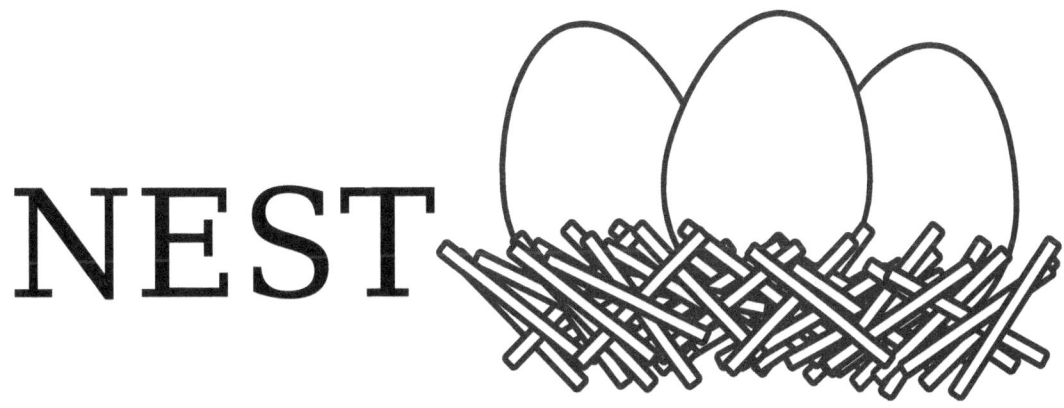

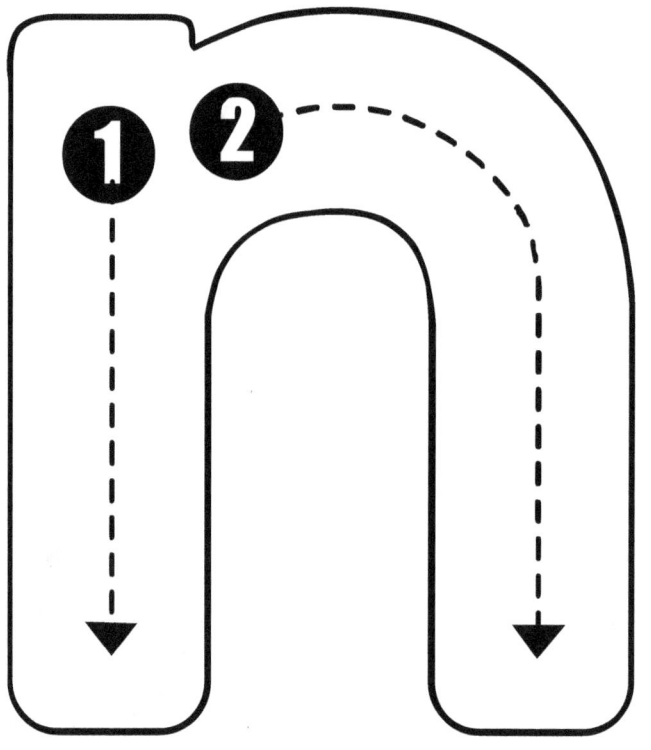

nest

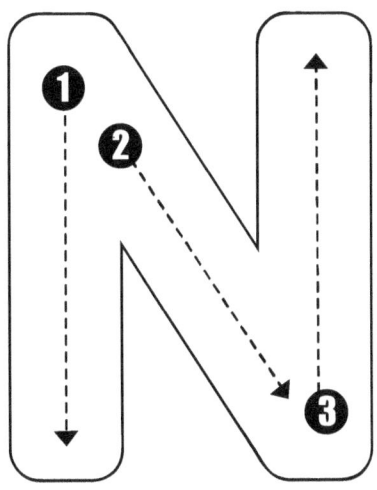 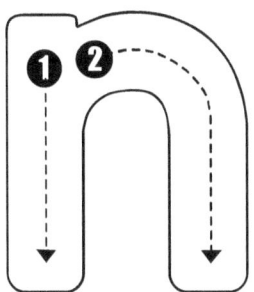

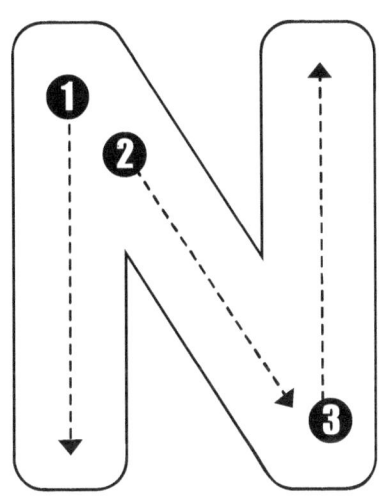 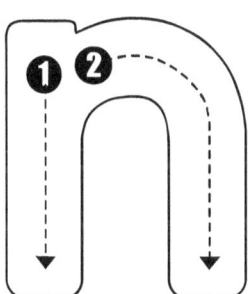

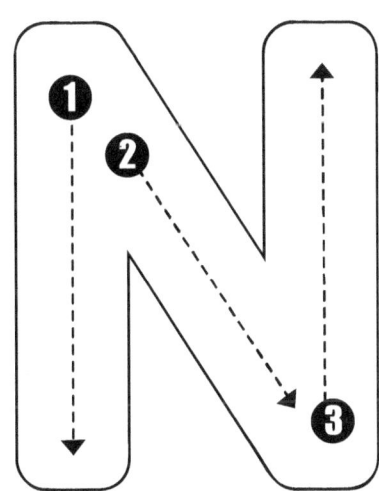 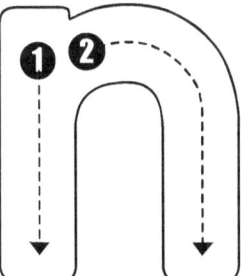

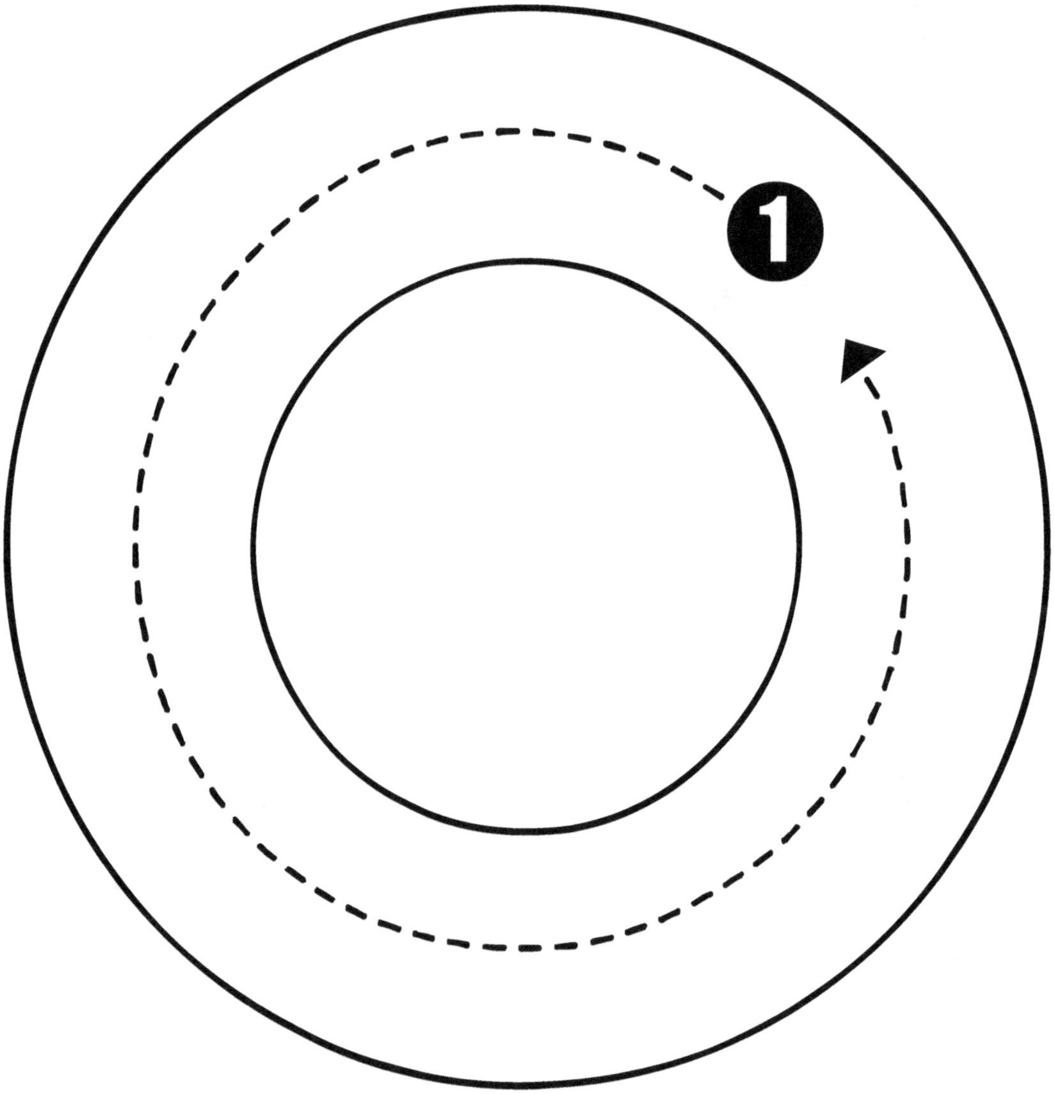

OWL

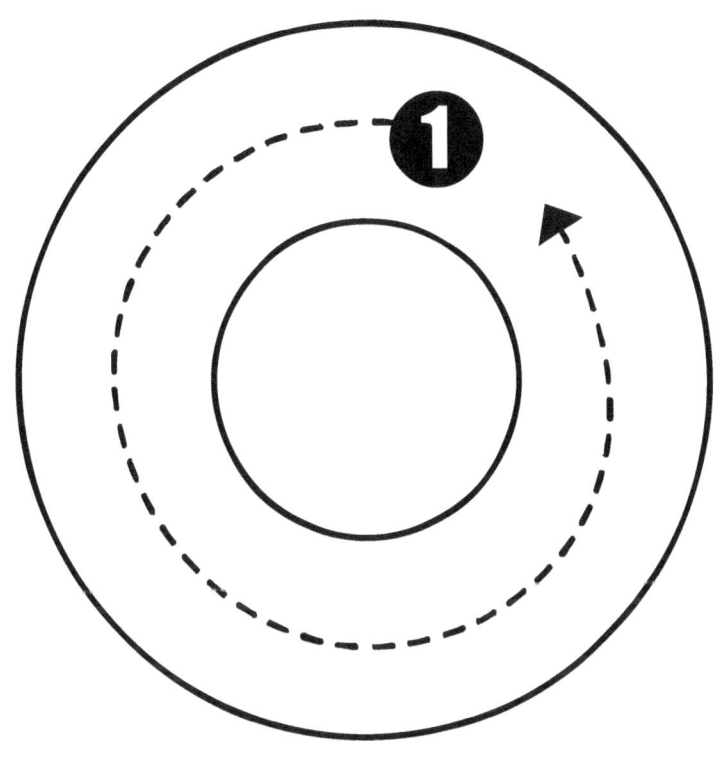

owl

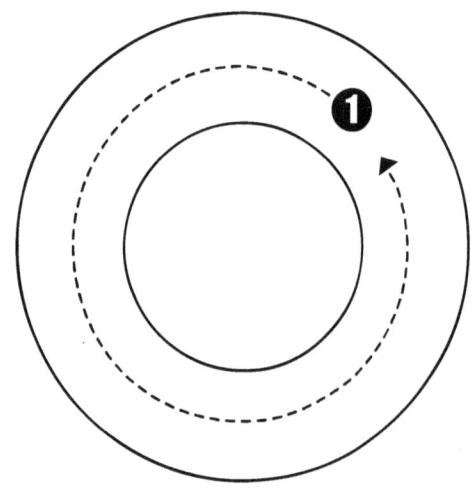
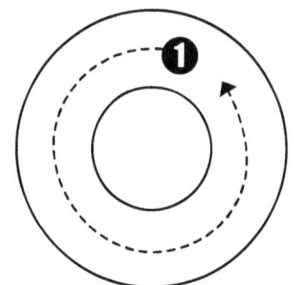
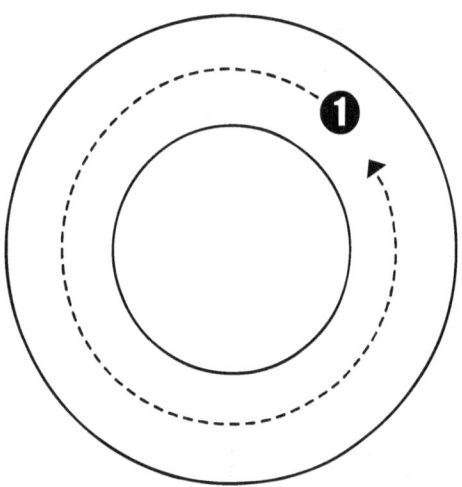
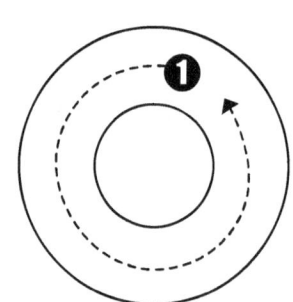
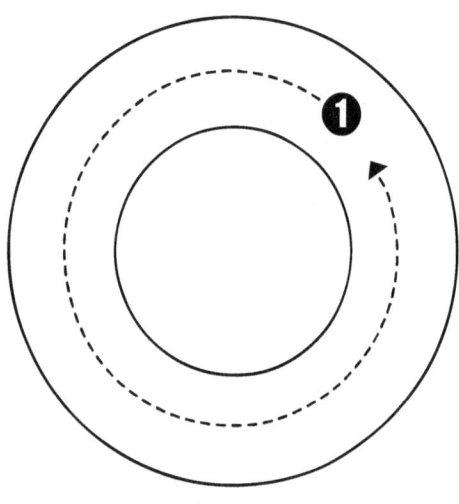
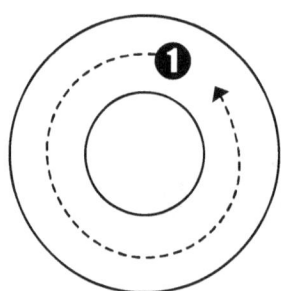

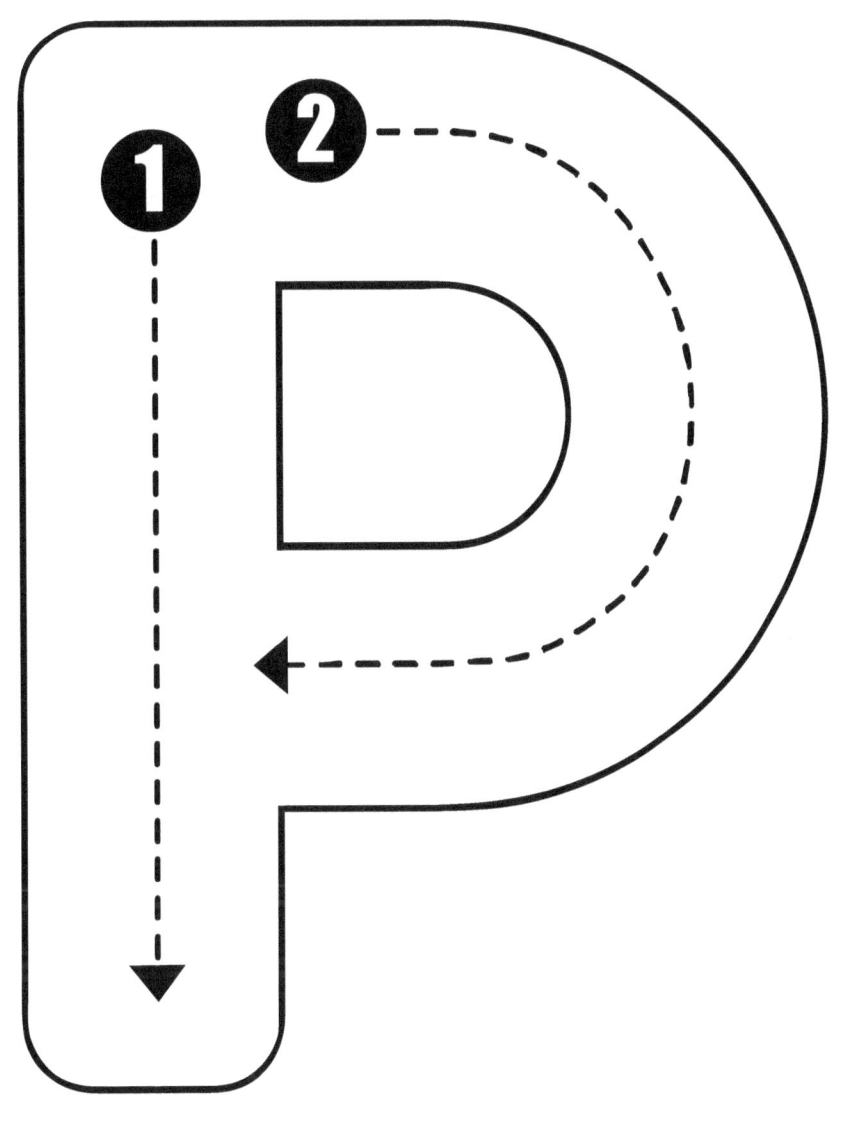

PIG

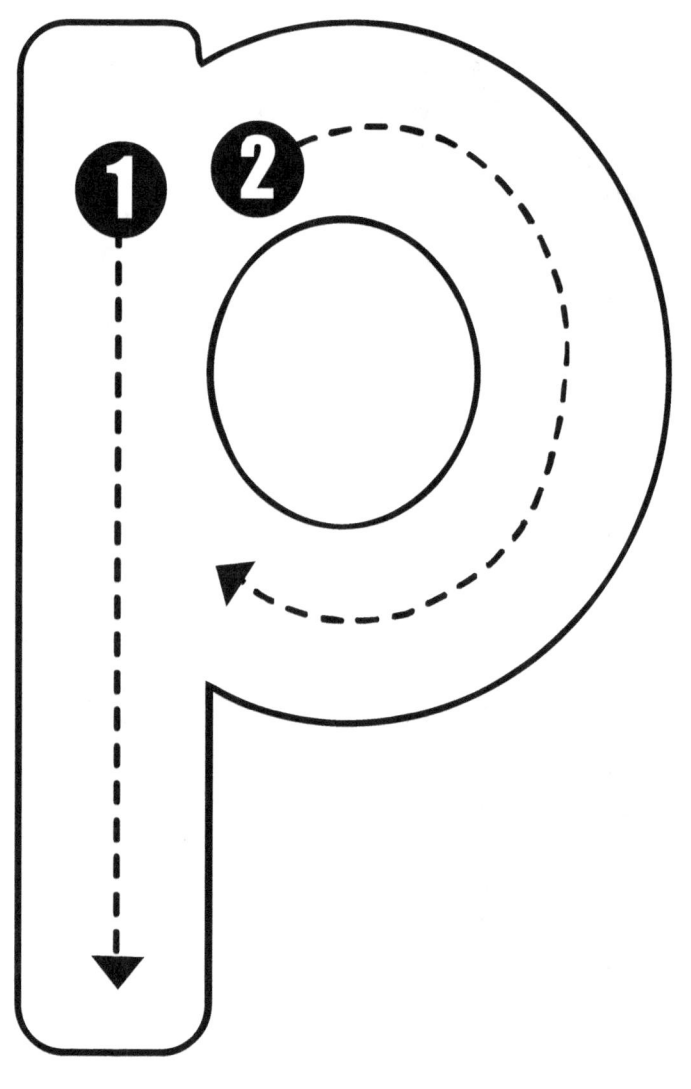

pig

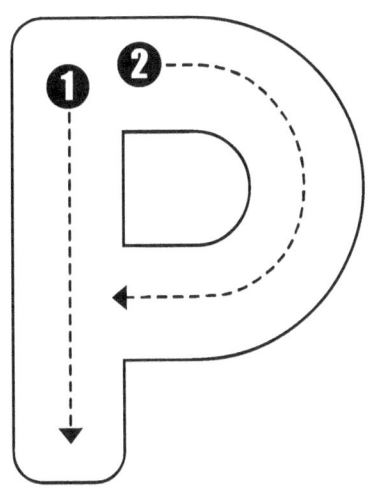 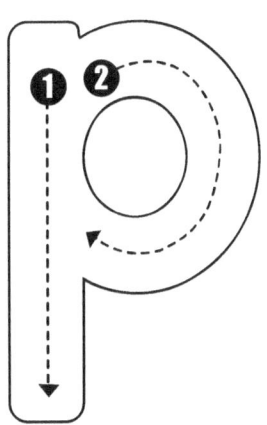

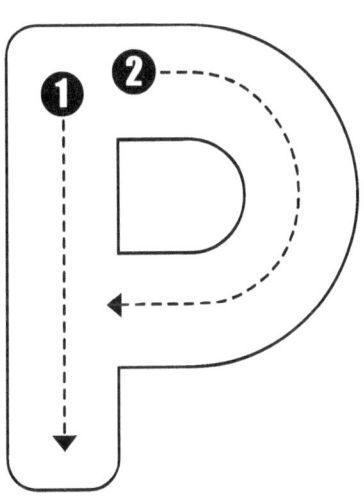 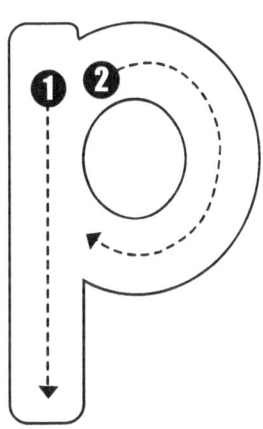

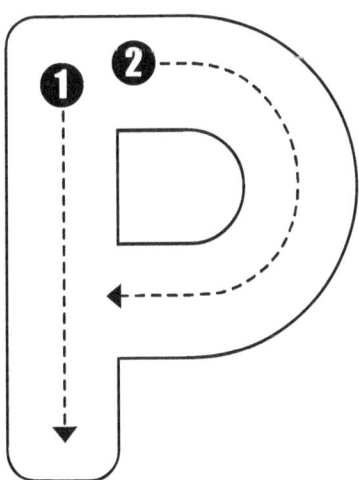 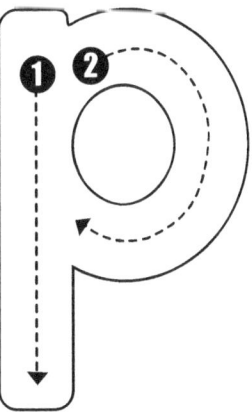

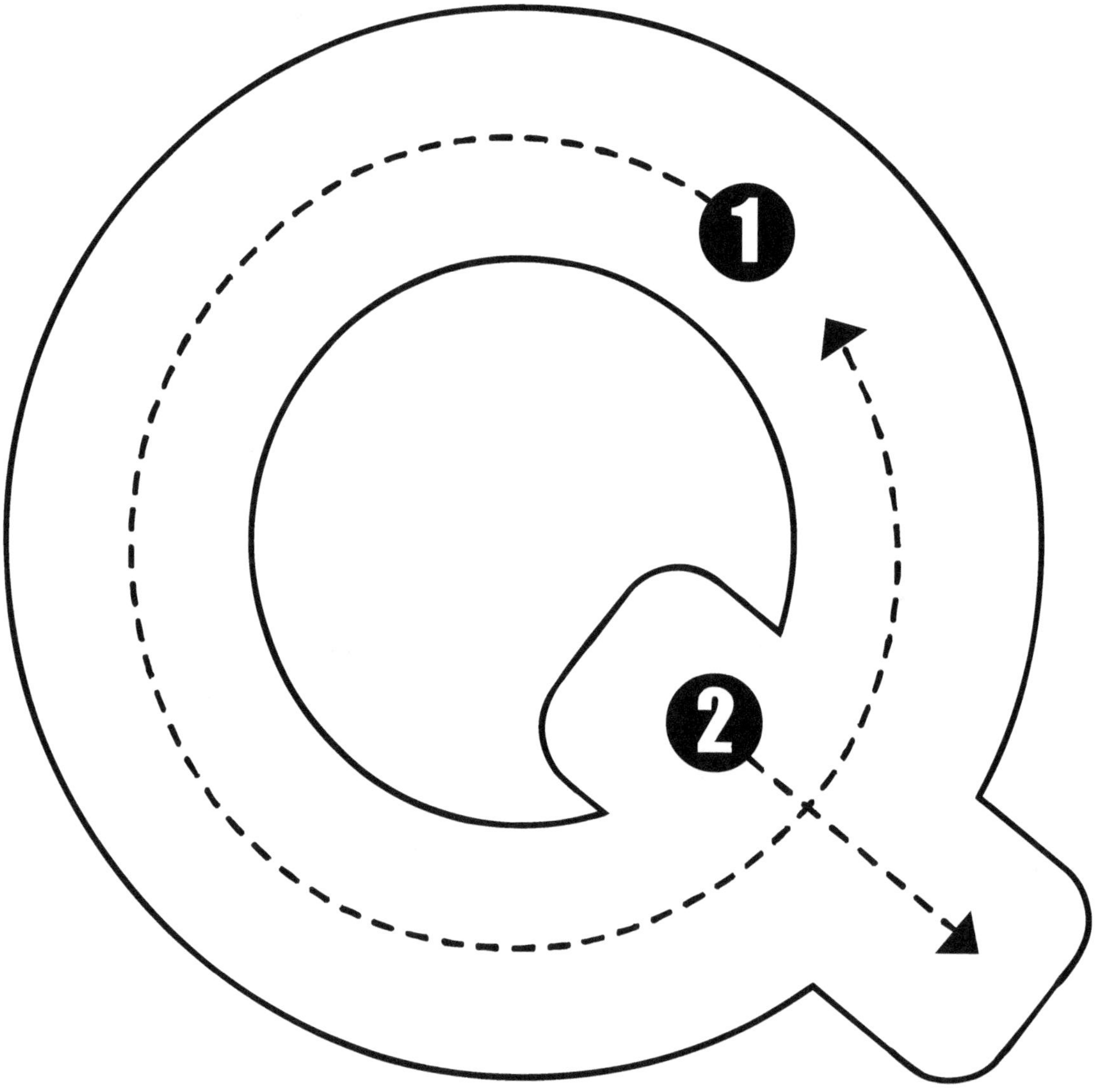

Q

QUEEN

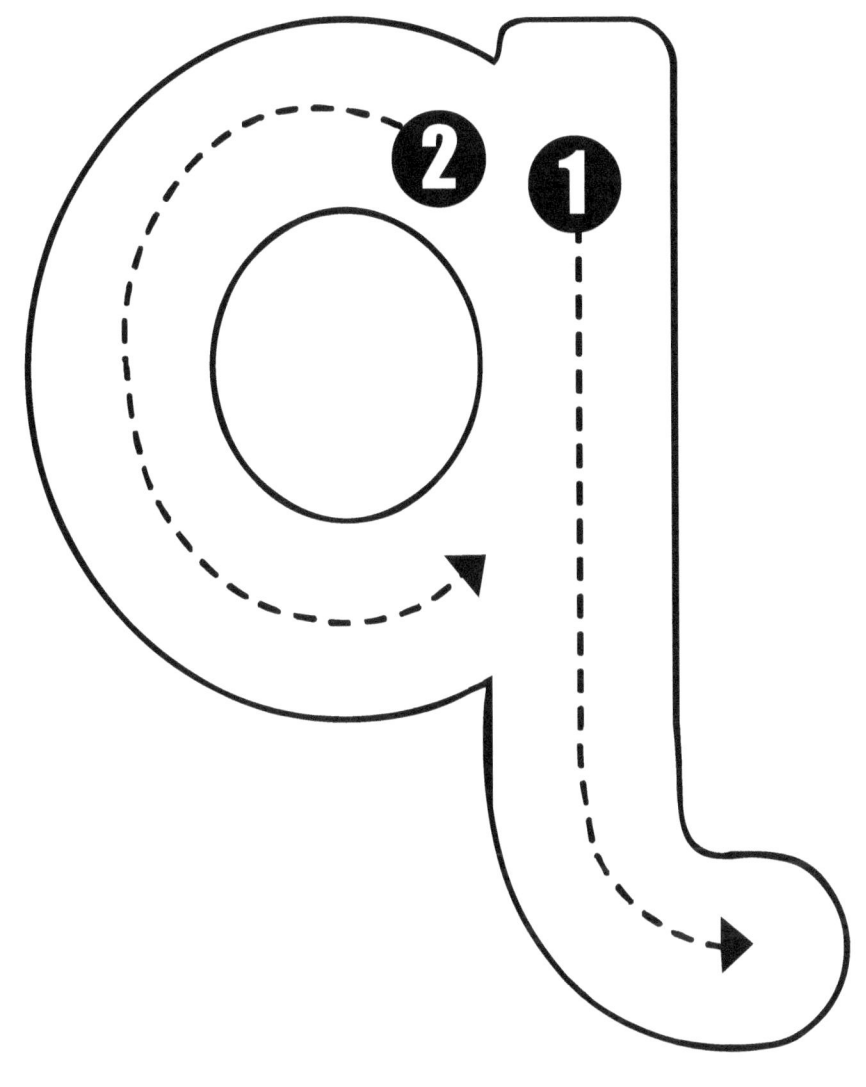

queen

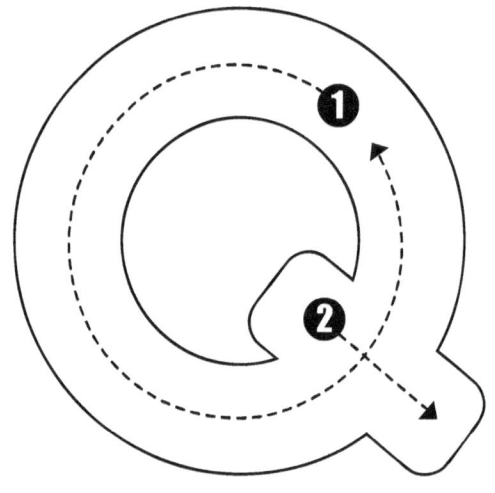 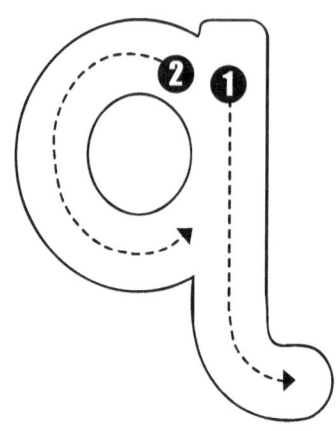

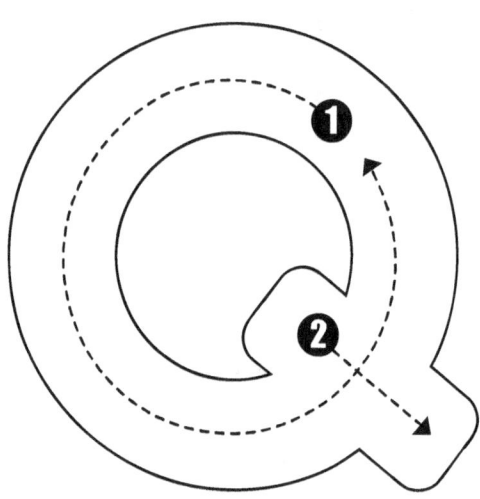 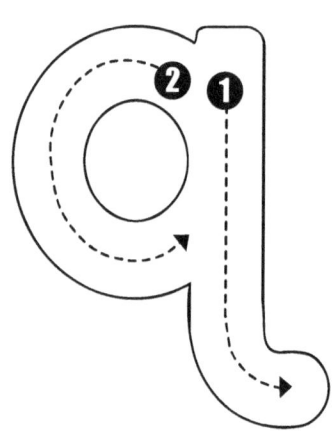

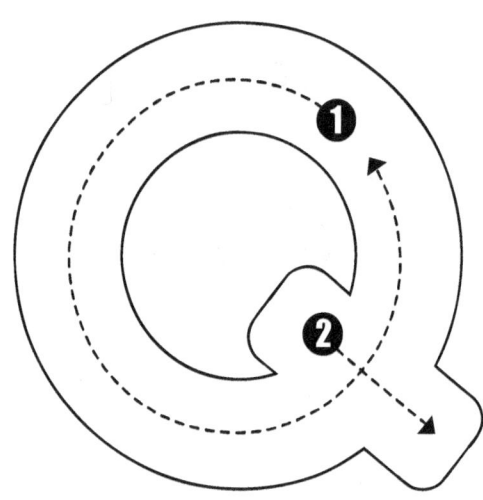 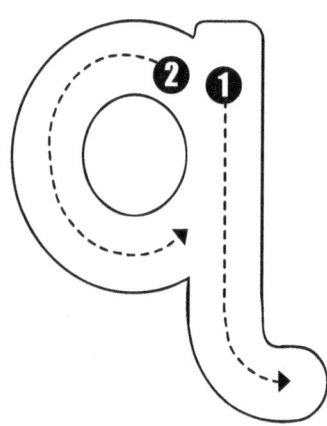

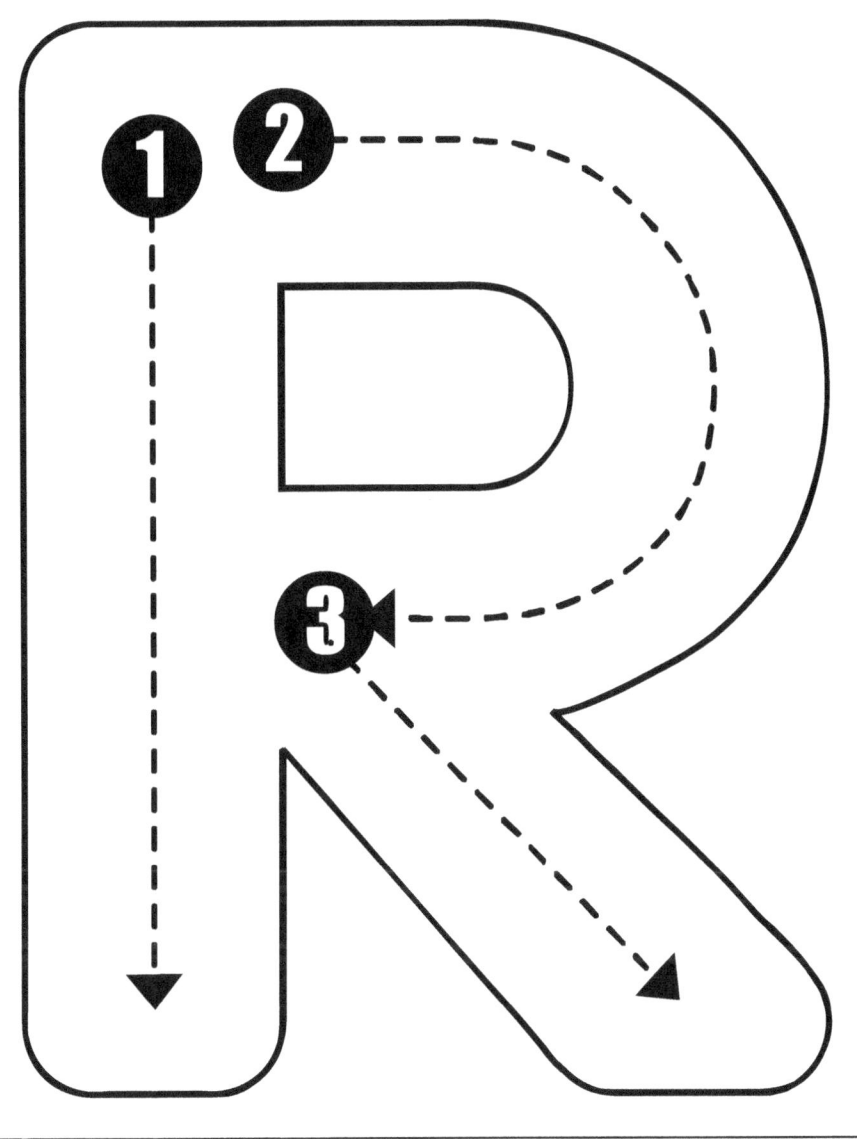

RABBIT

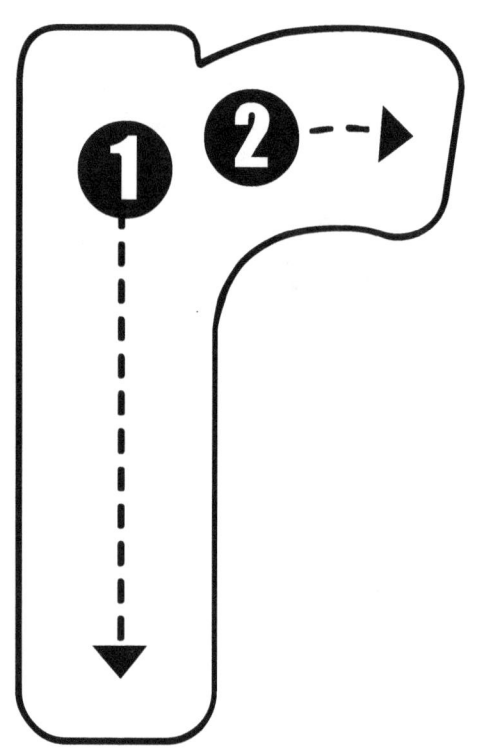

rabbit

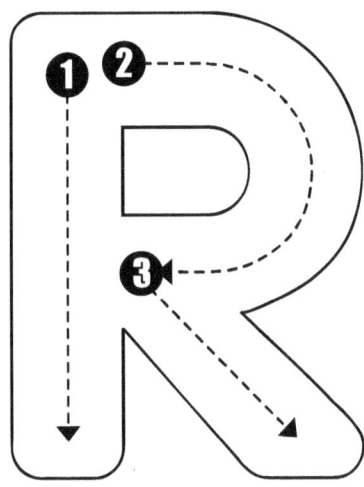 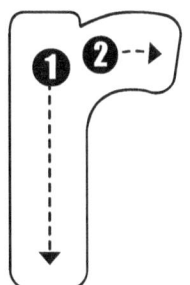

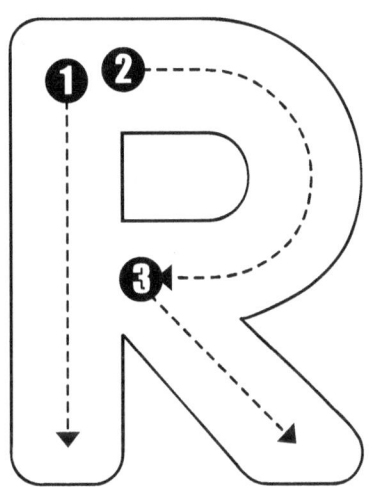 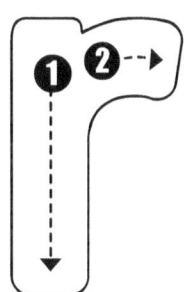

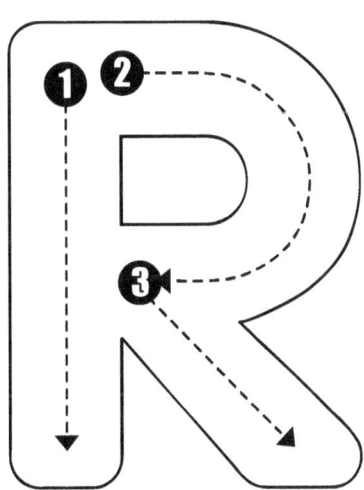 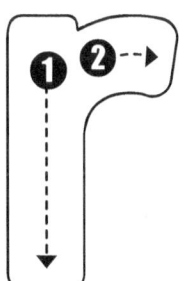

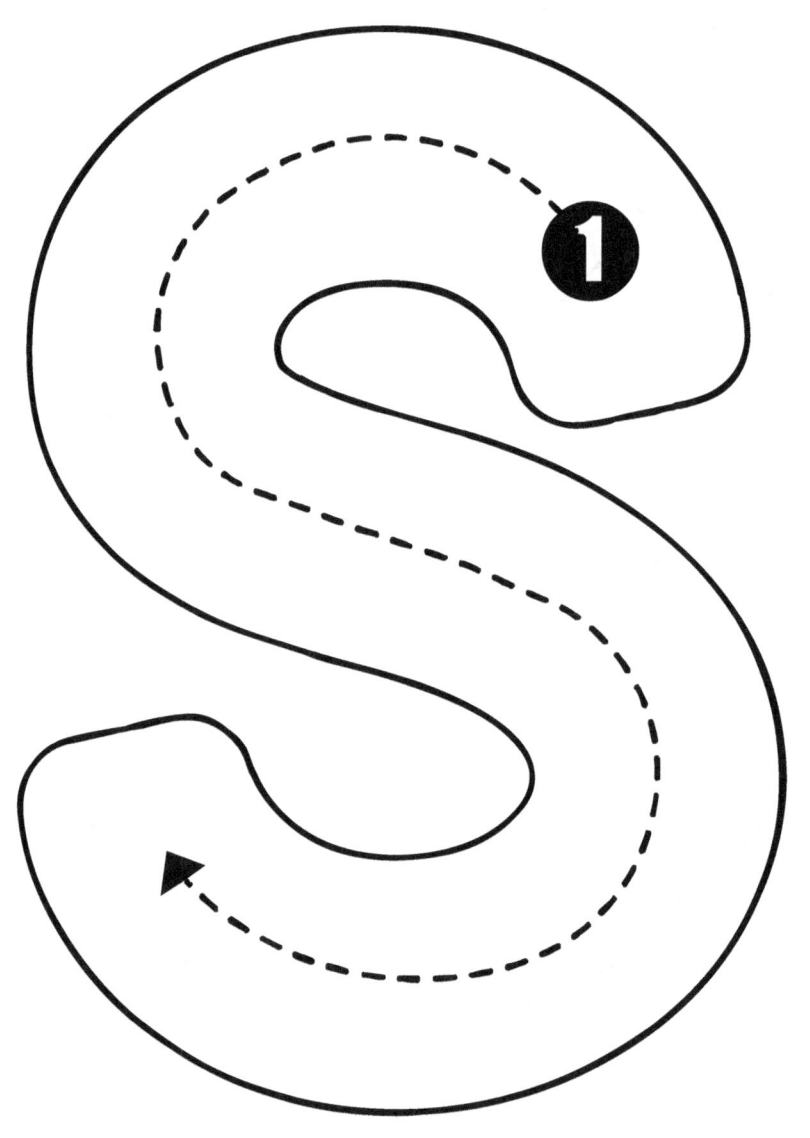

SNAIL

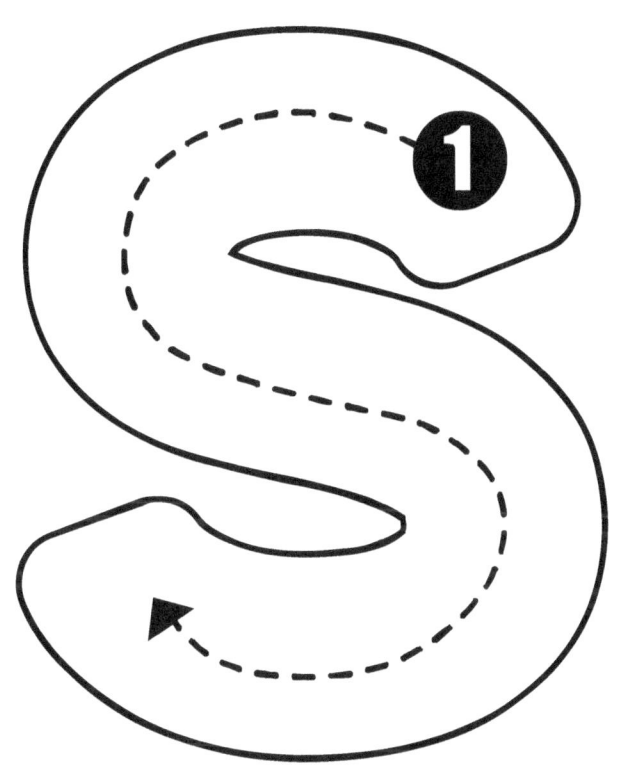

snail

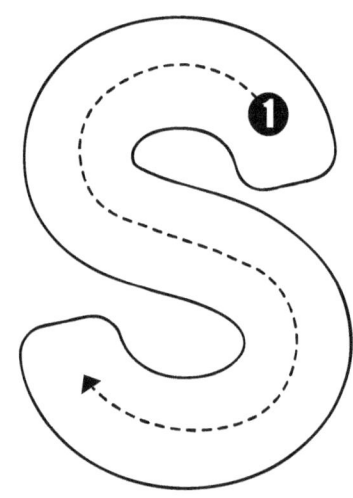 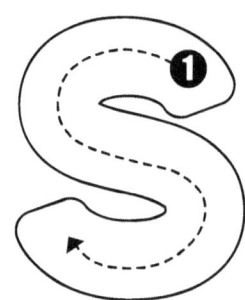

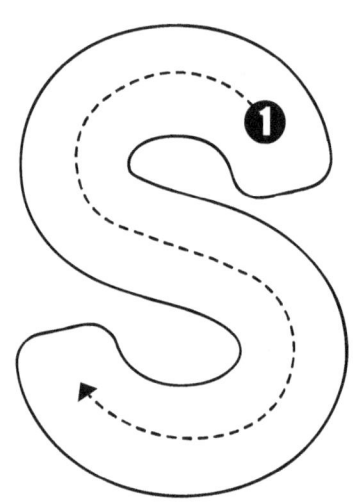 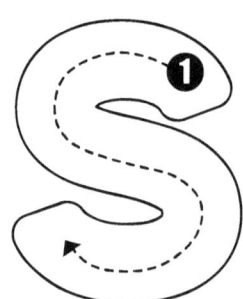

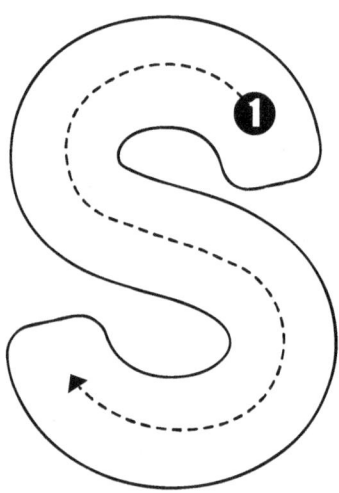 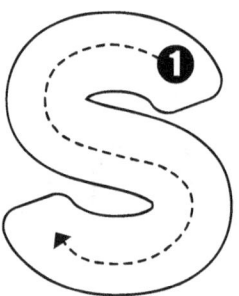

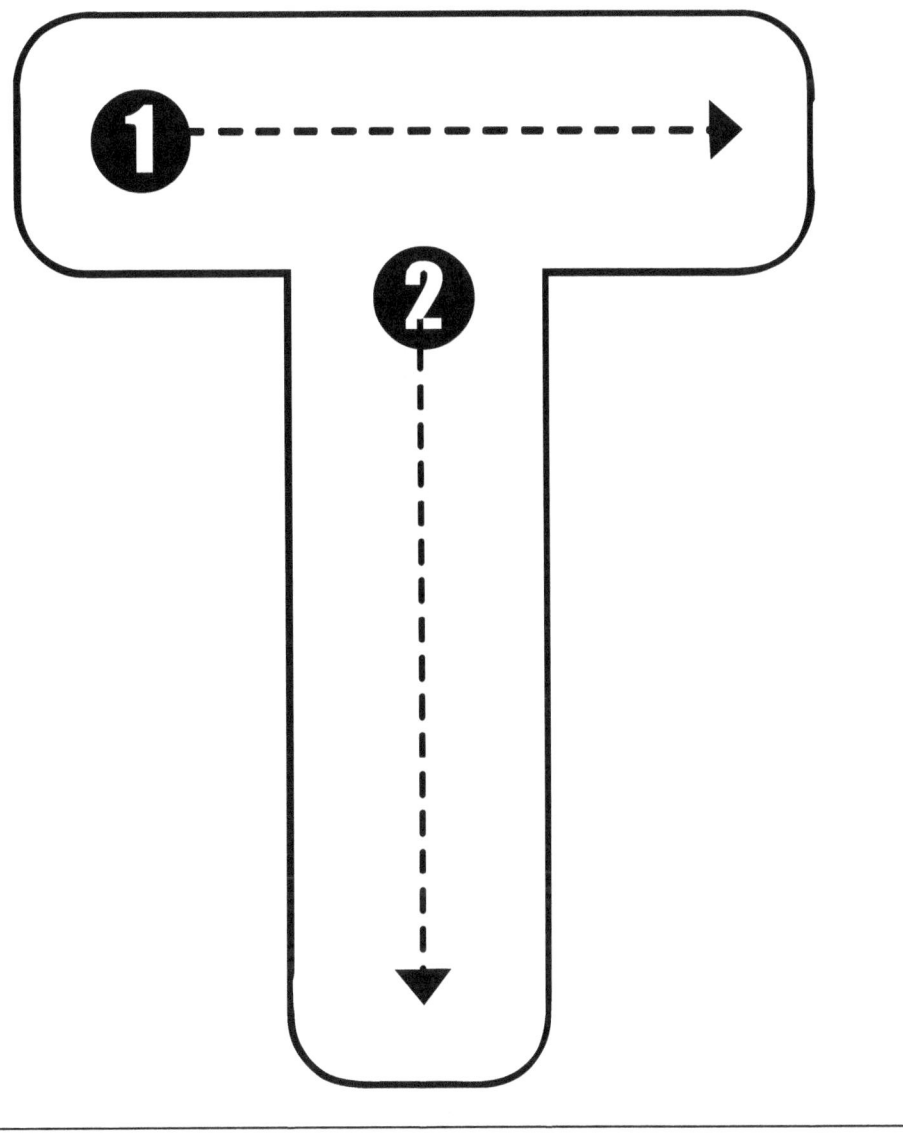

TURTLE

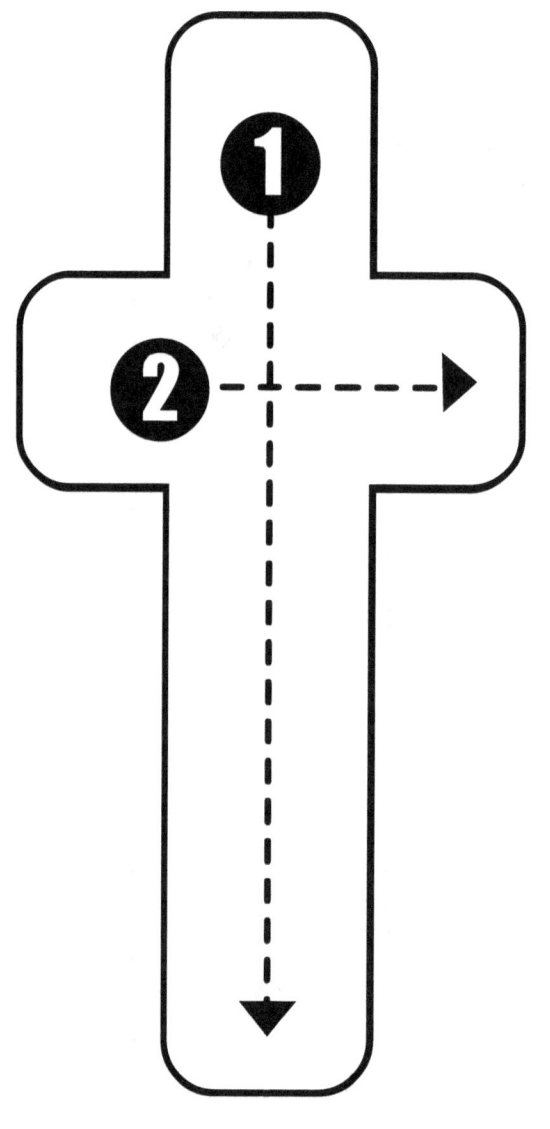

turtle

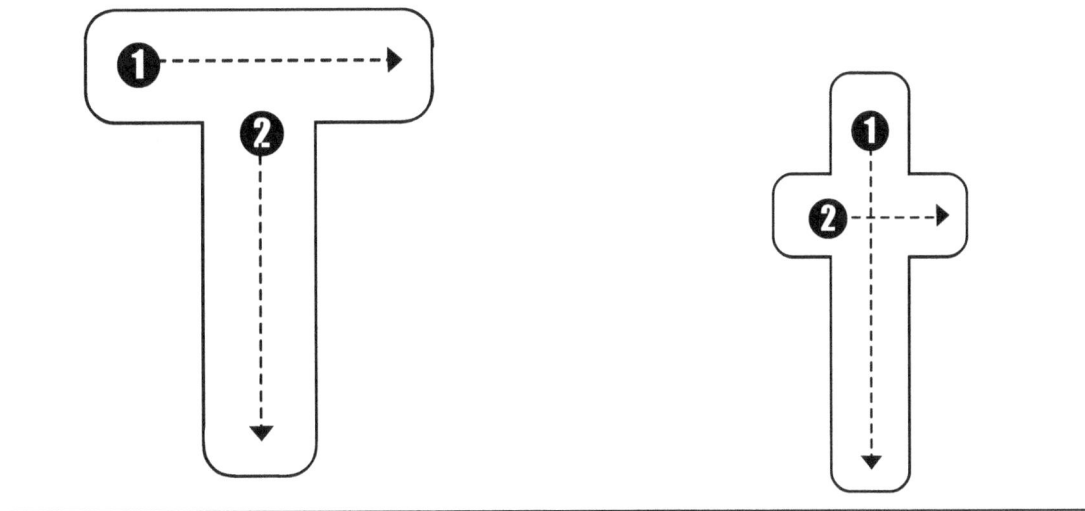
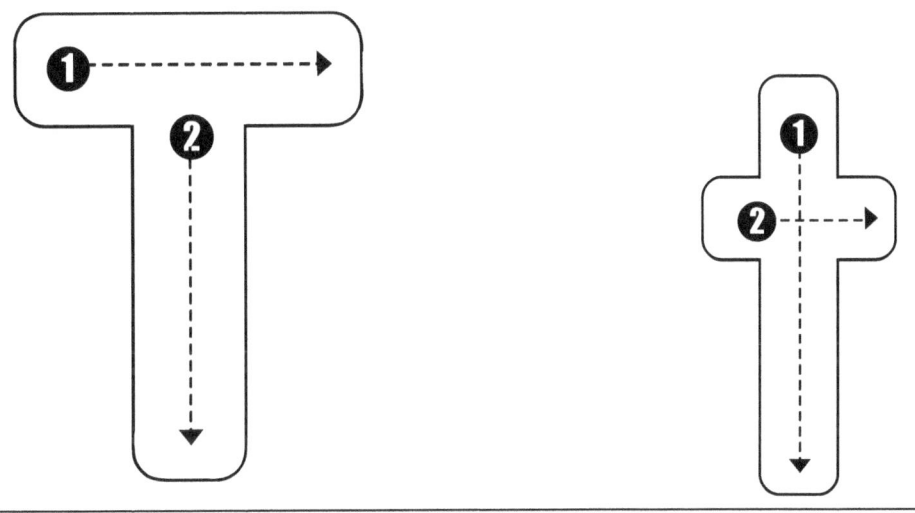
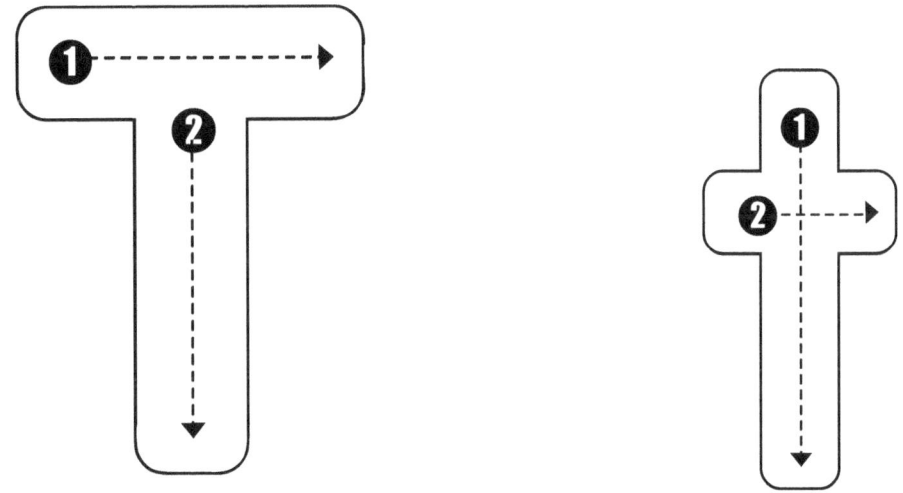

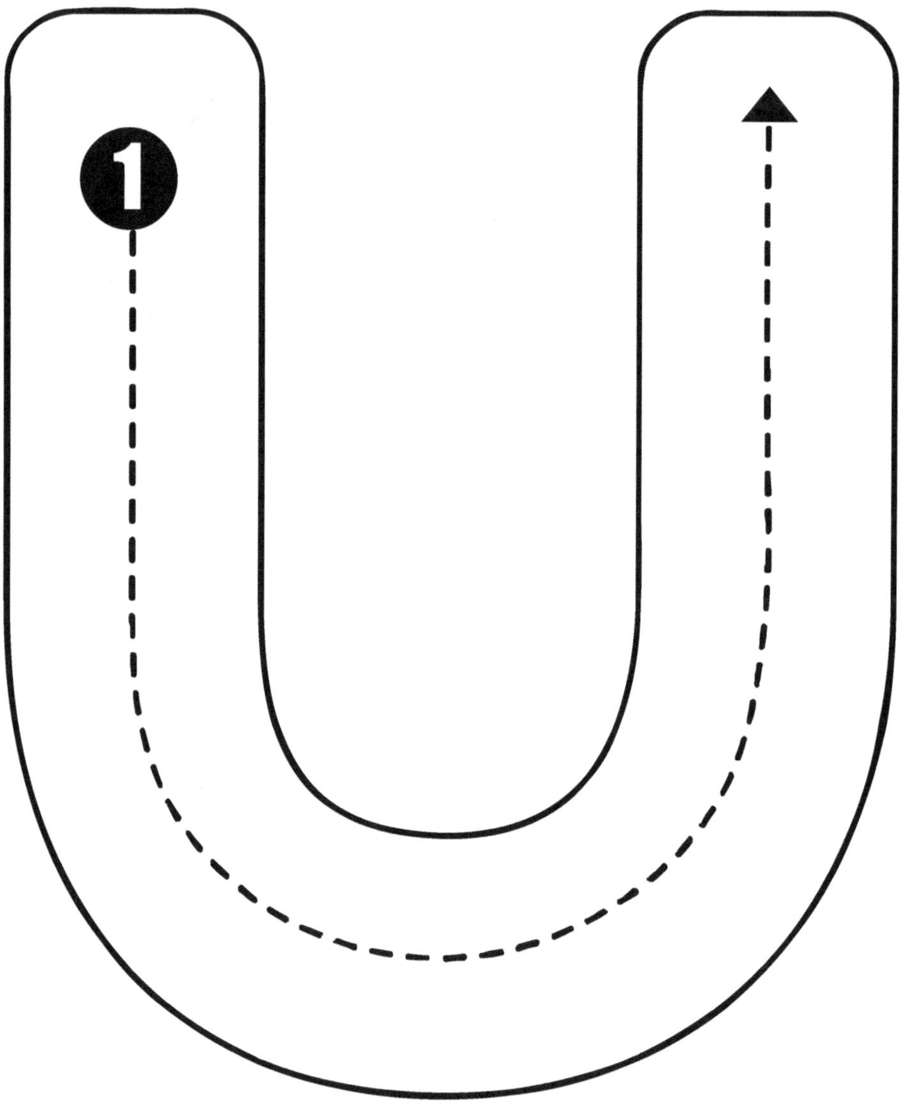

UNICORN

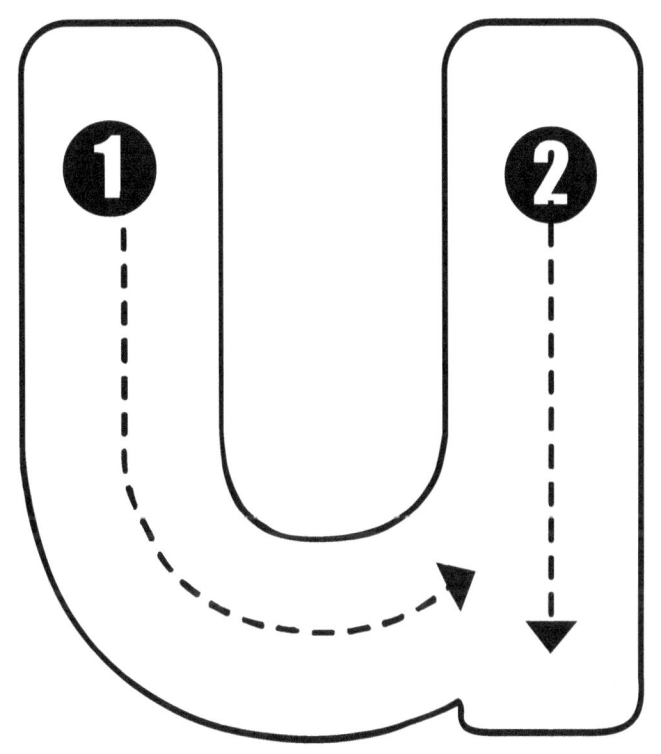

unicorn

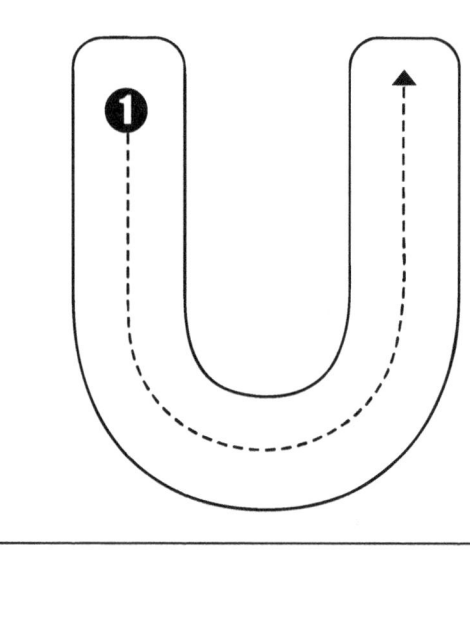 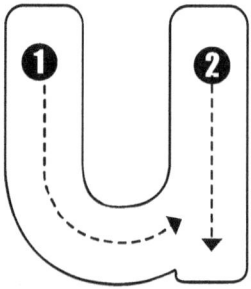

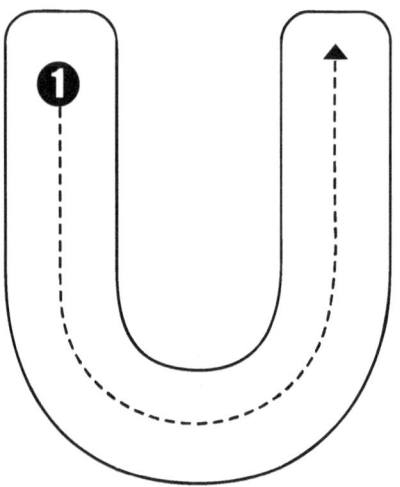 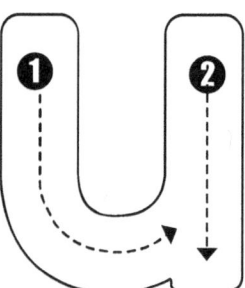

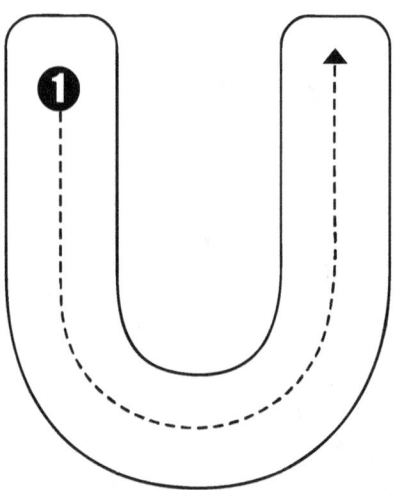 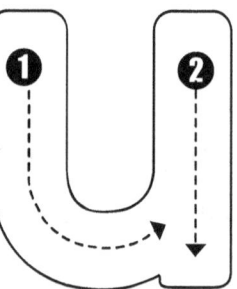

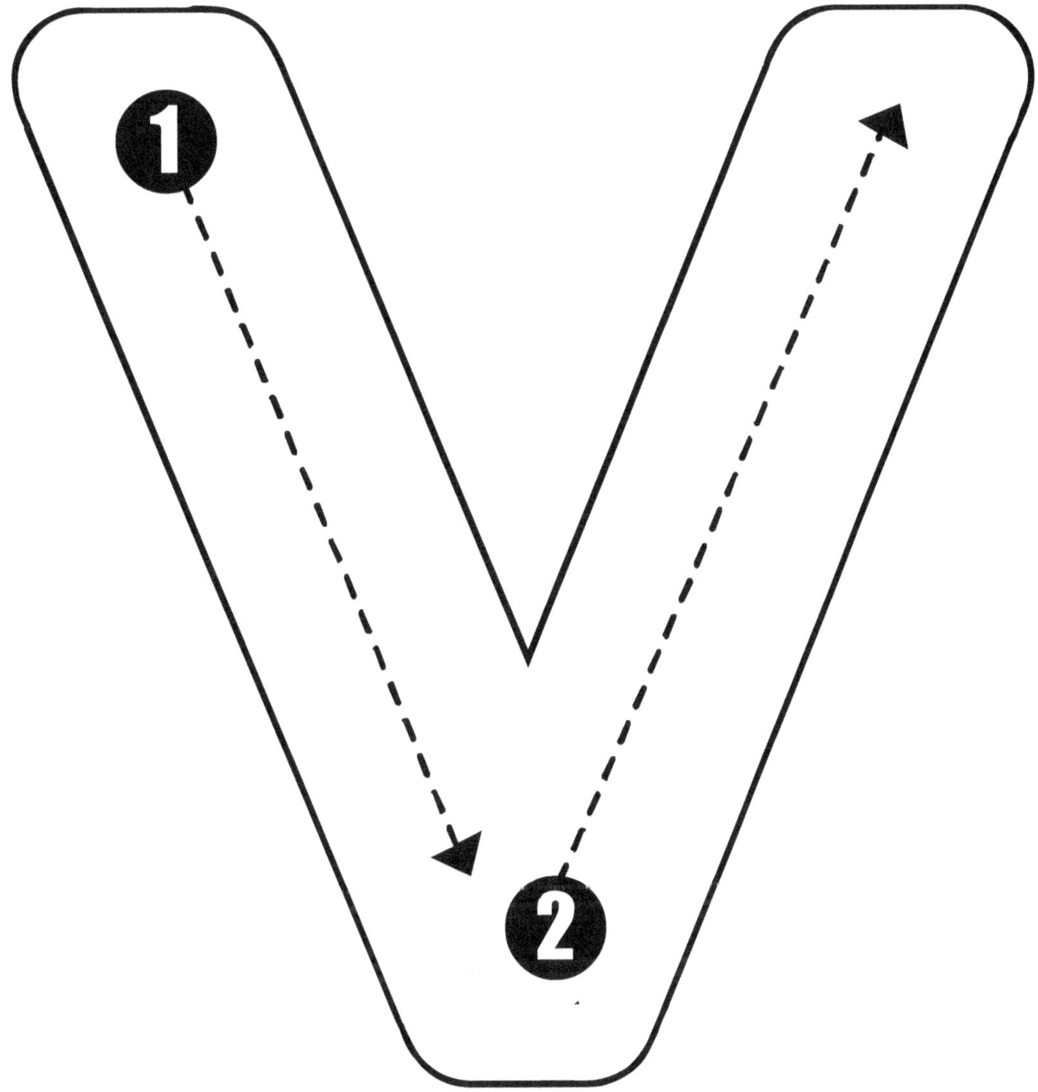

VASE

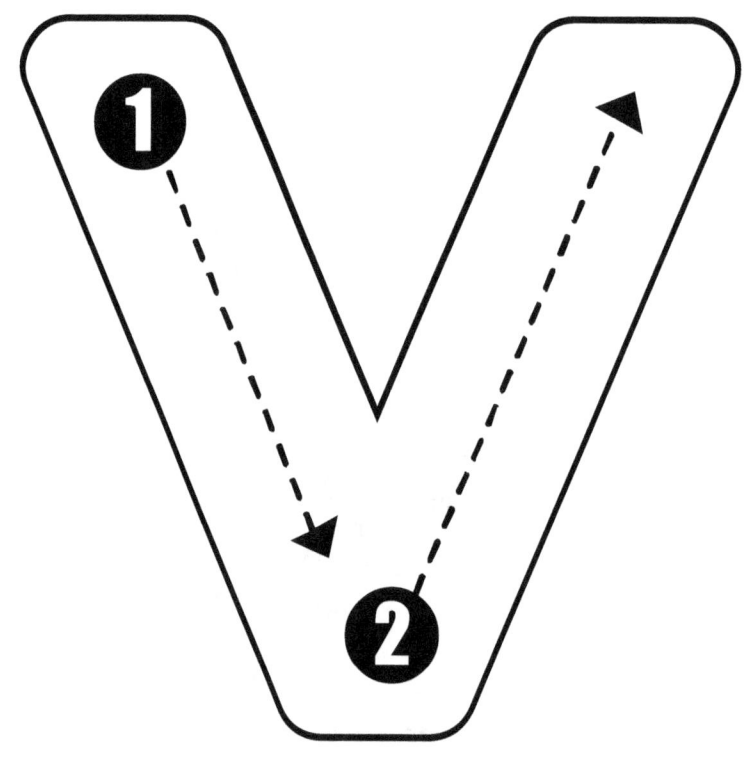

vase

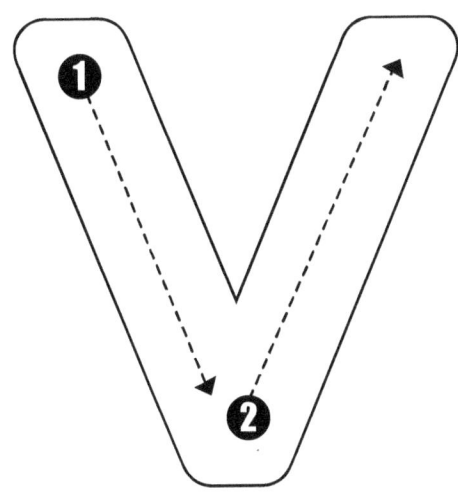 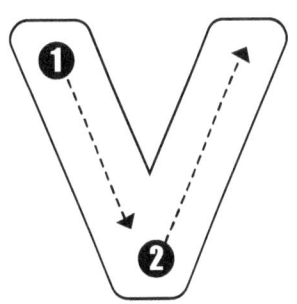

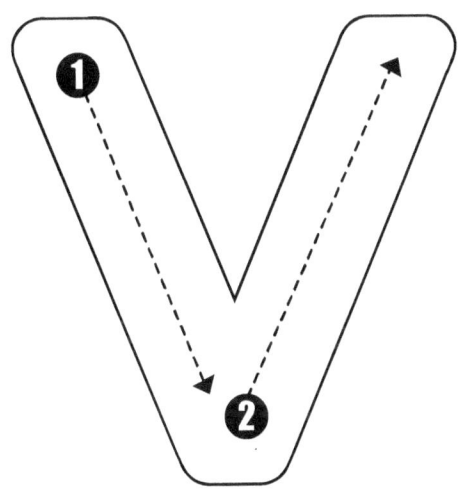 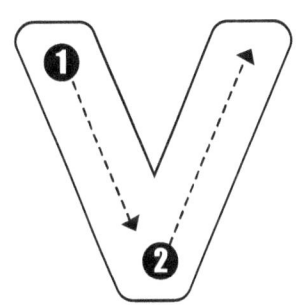

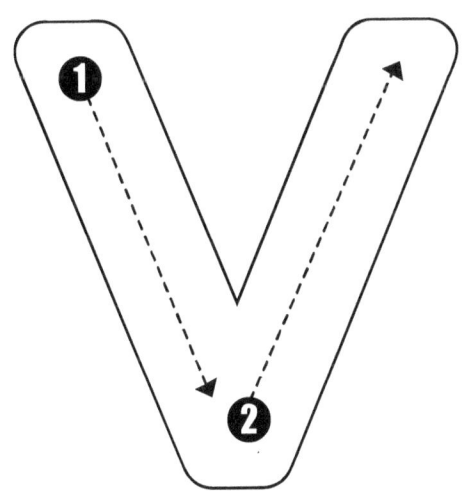 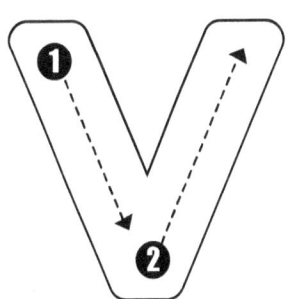

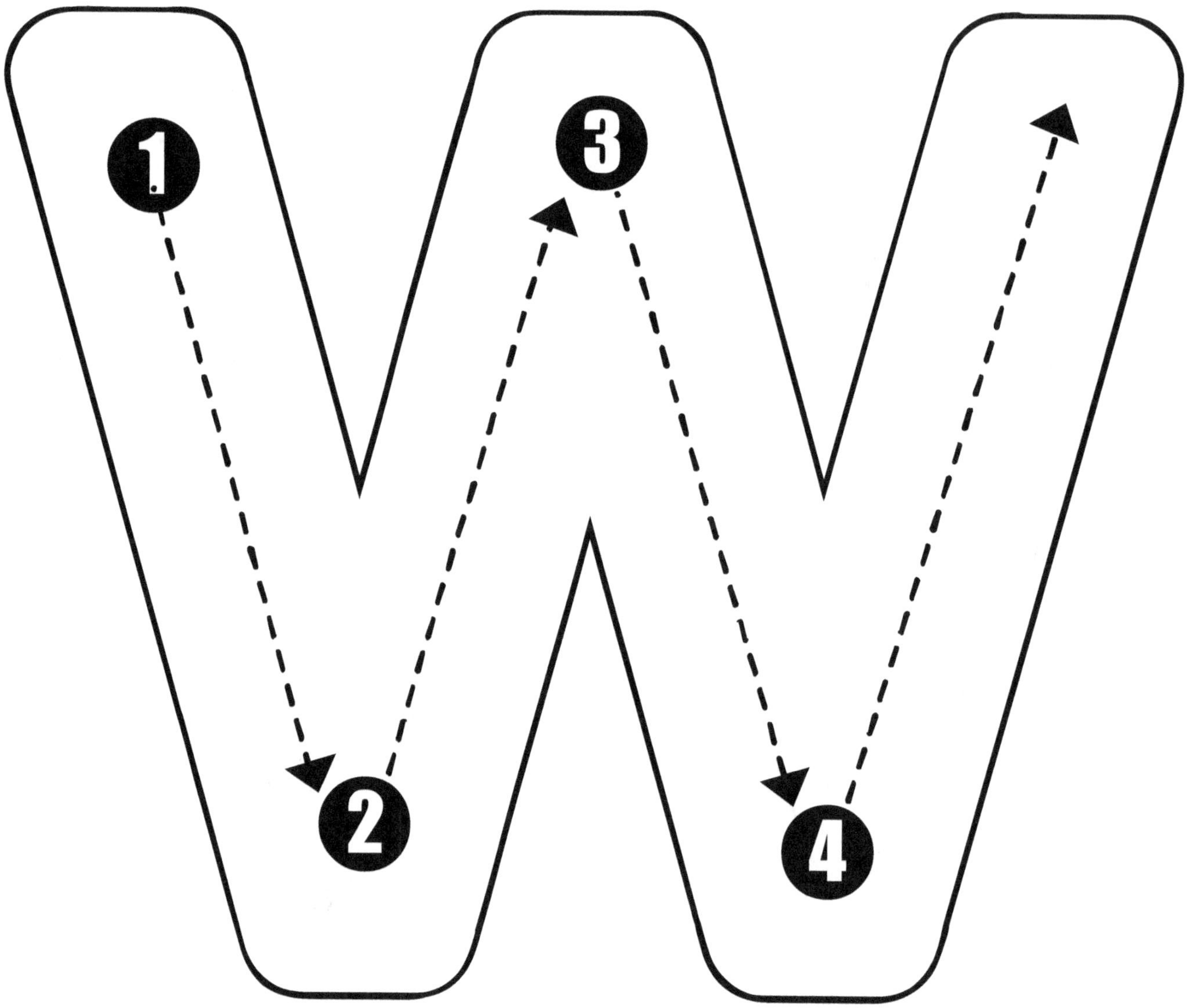

W

WHALE

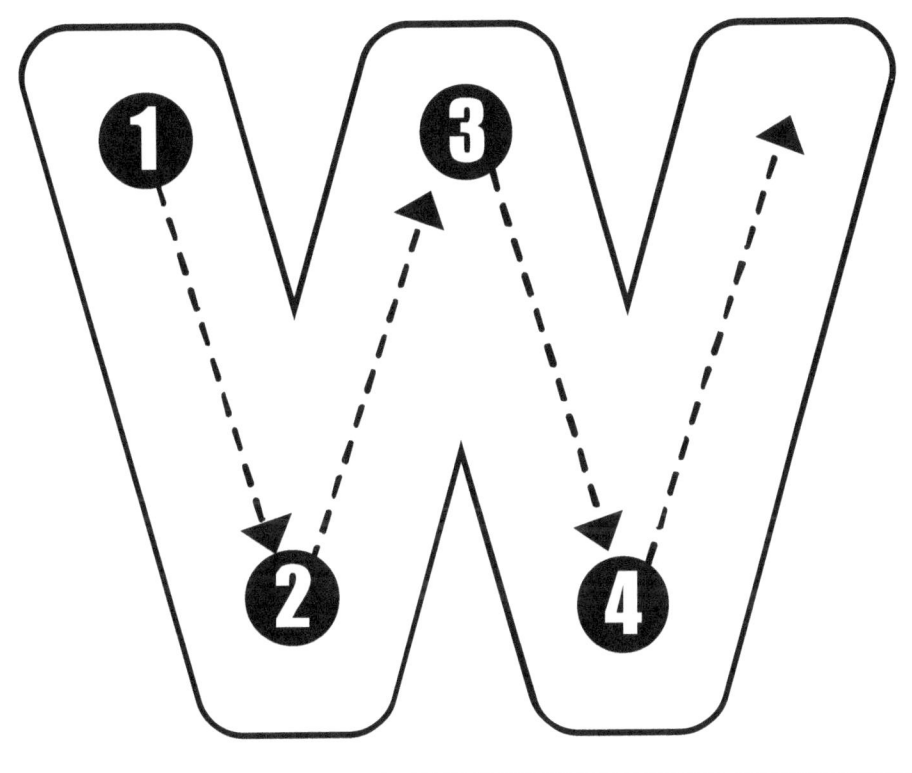

whale

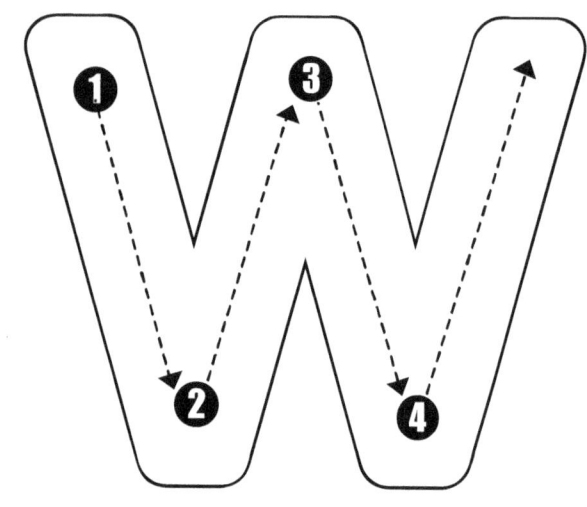
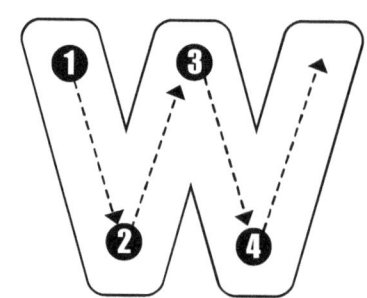
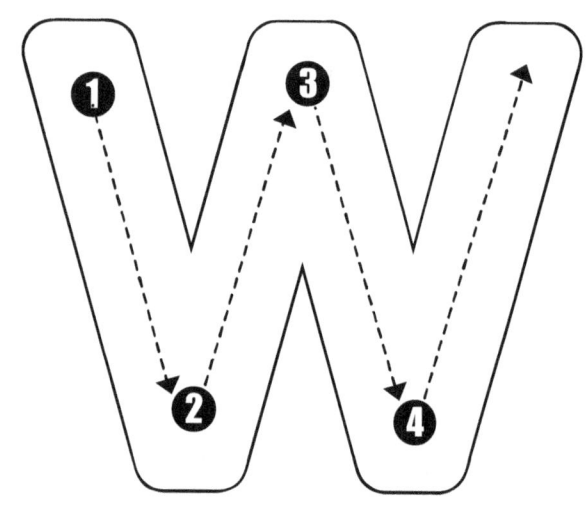
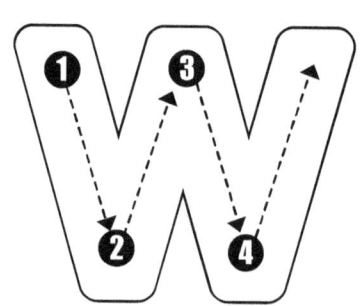
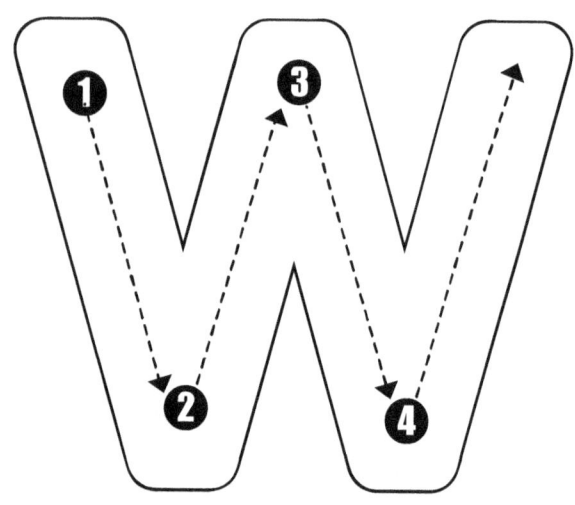
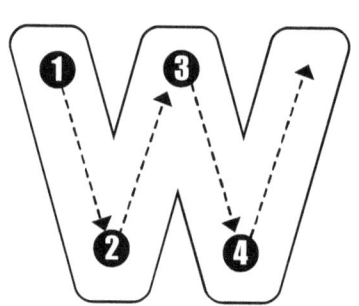

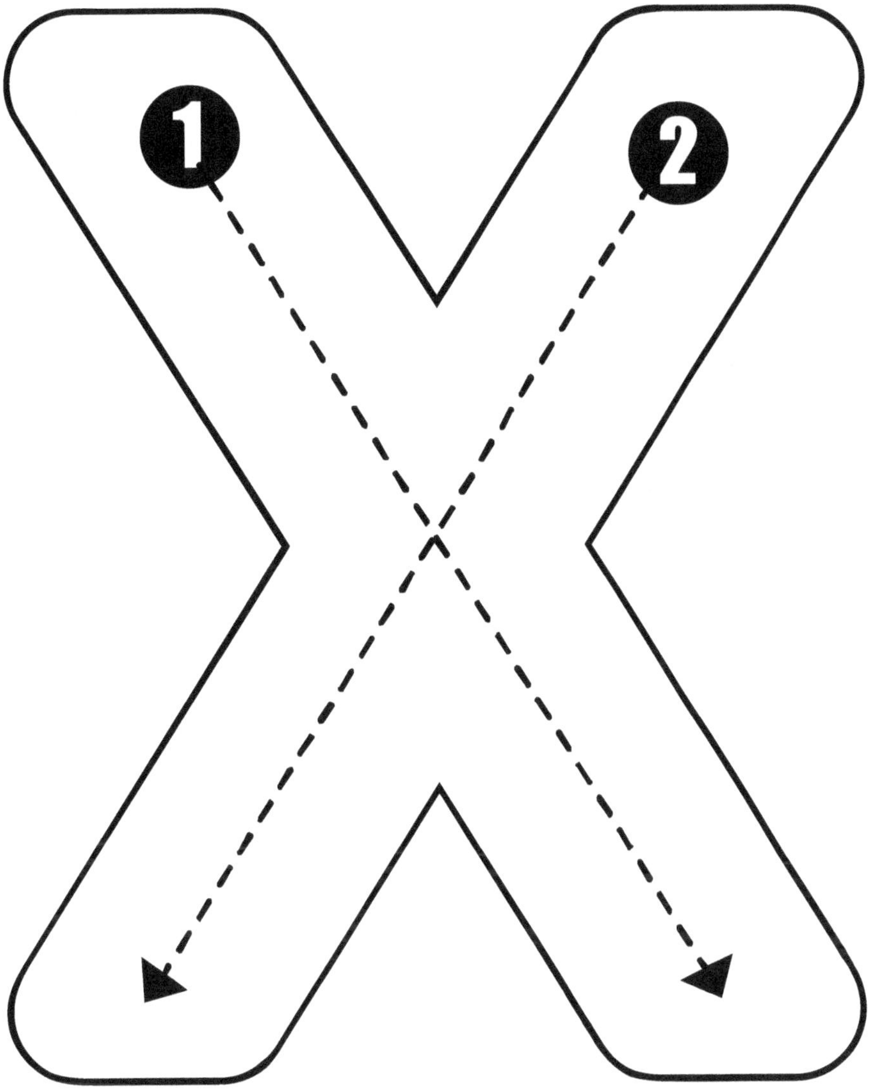

XYLOPHONE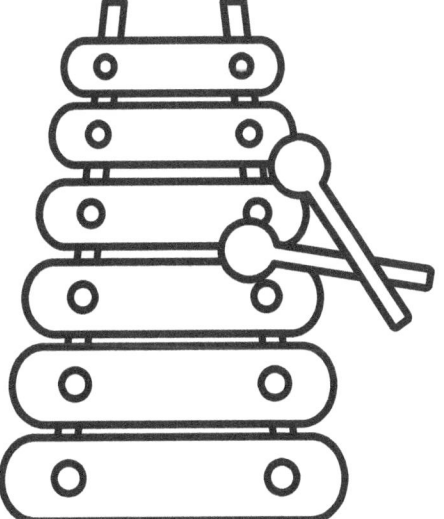

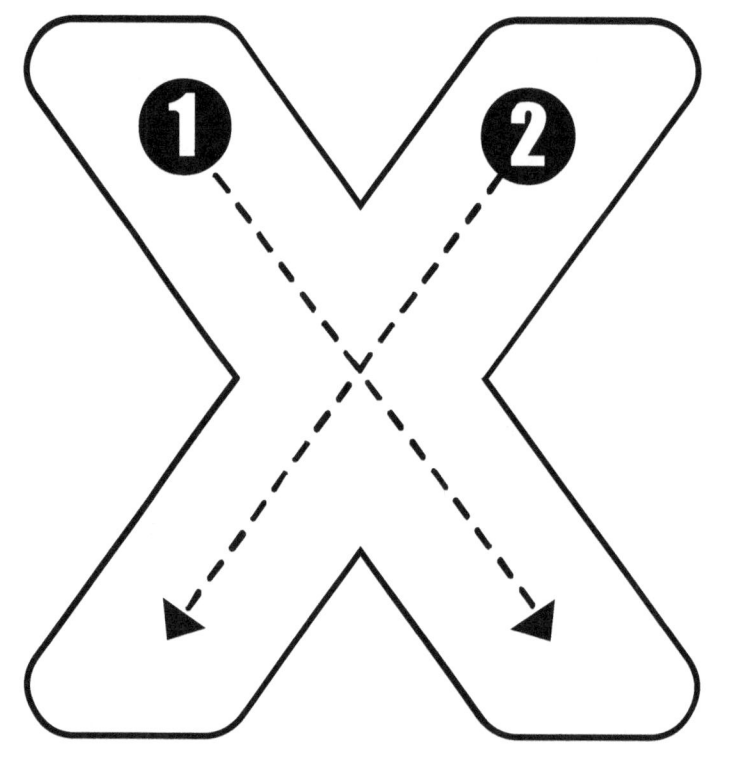

xylophone

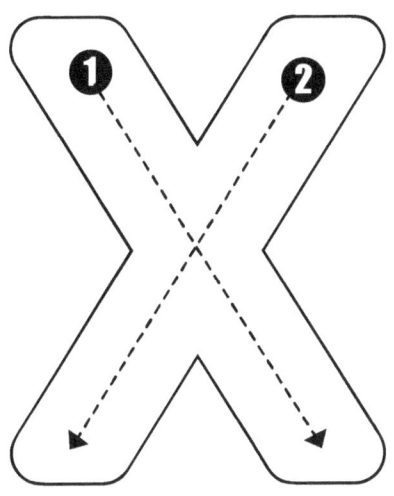 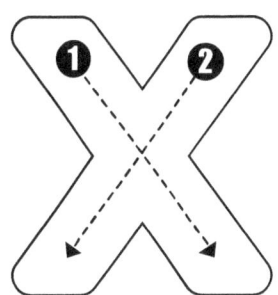

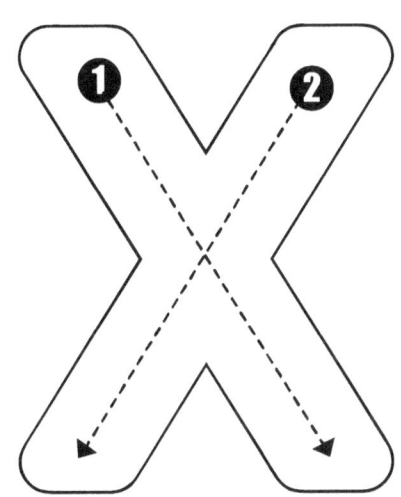 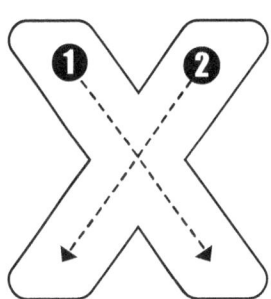

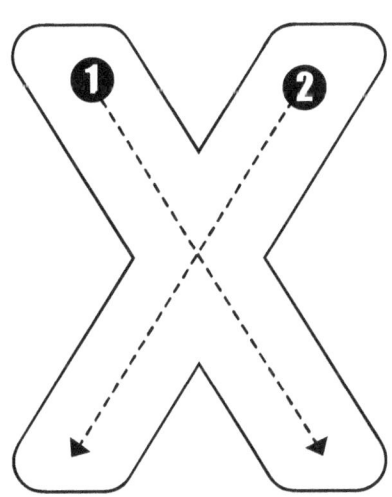 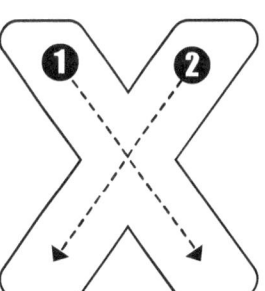

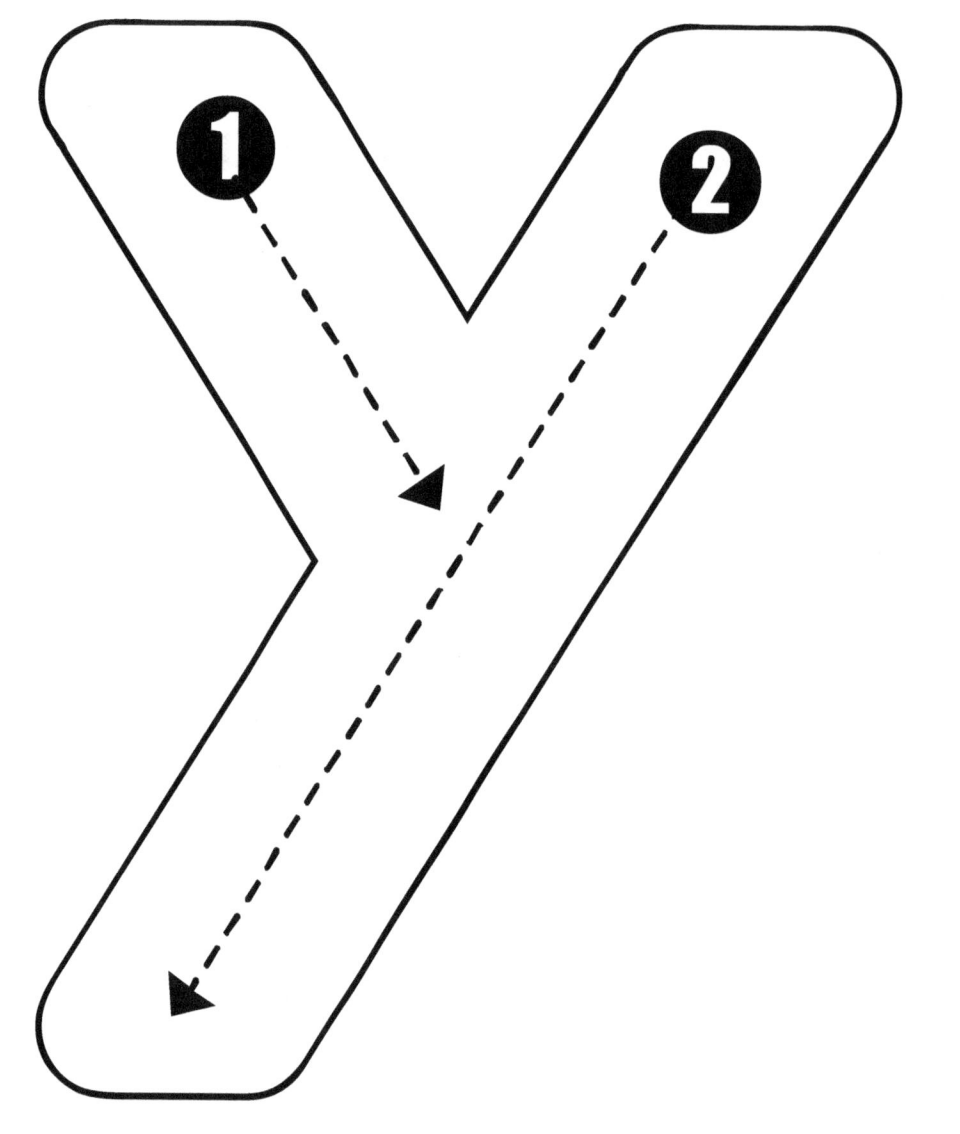

YACHT

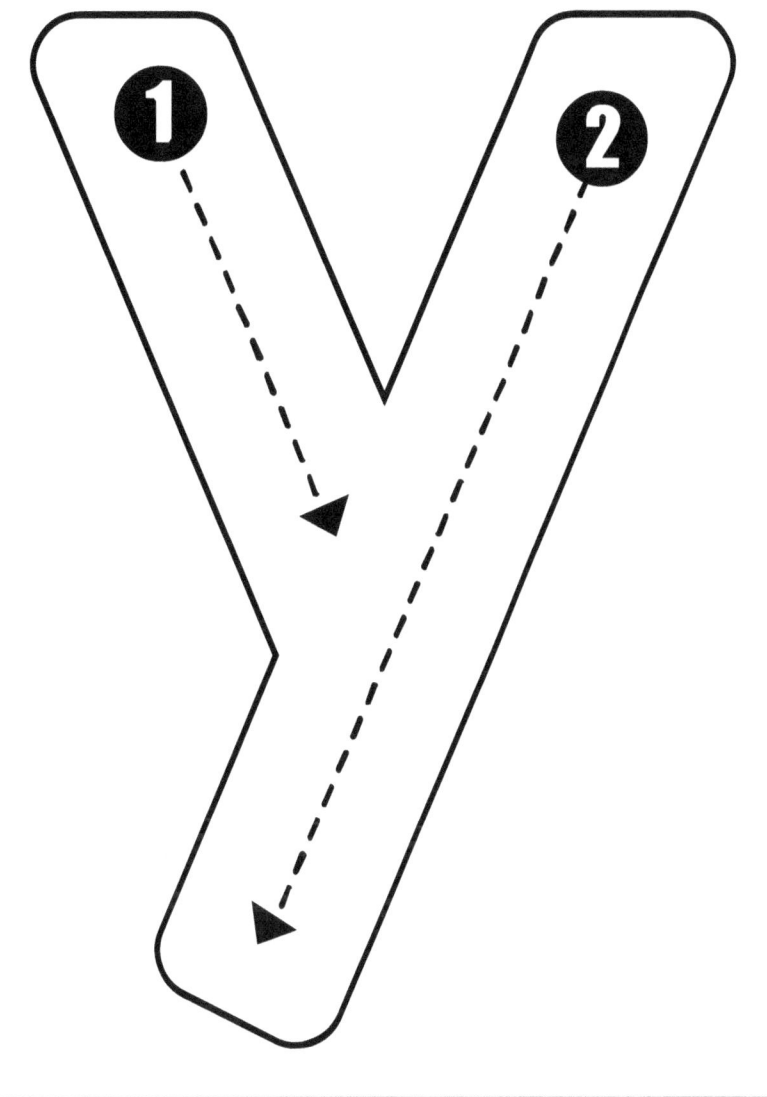

yacht

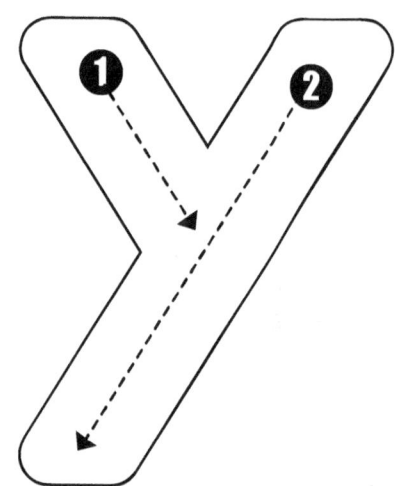 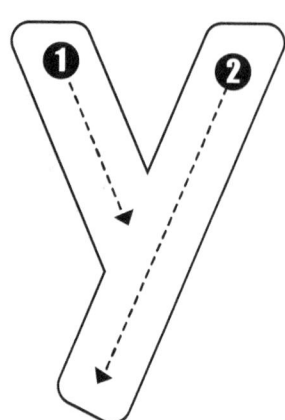

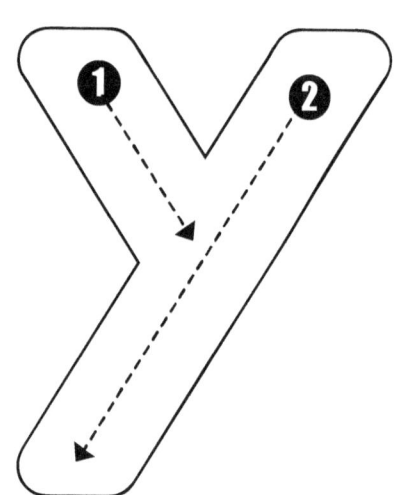 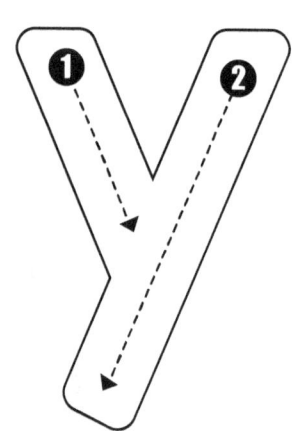

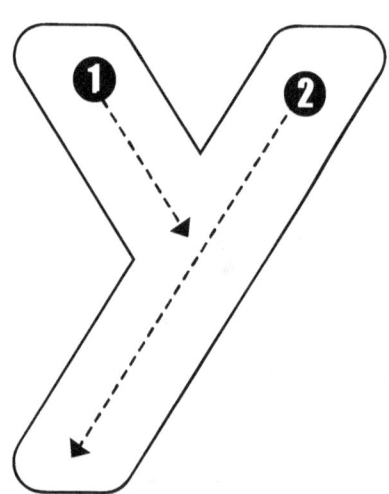 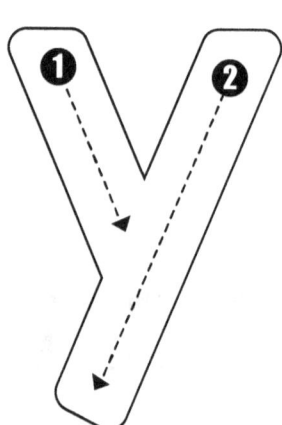

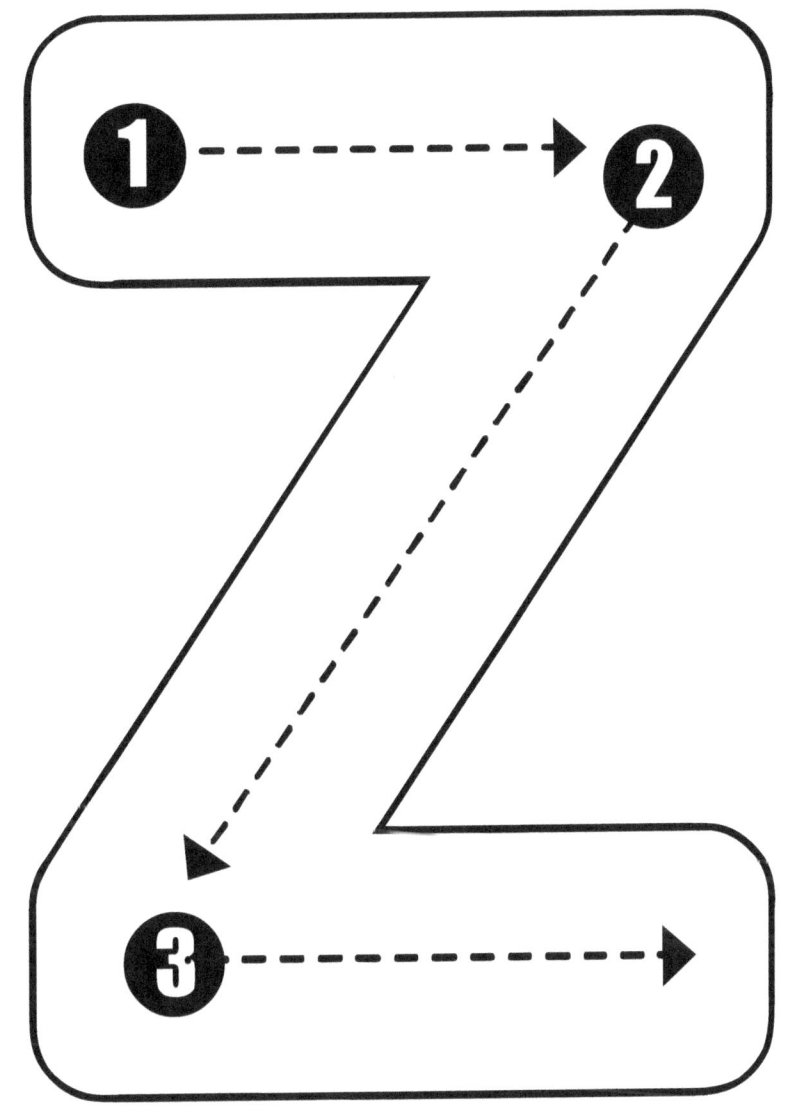

ZEBRA

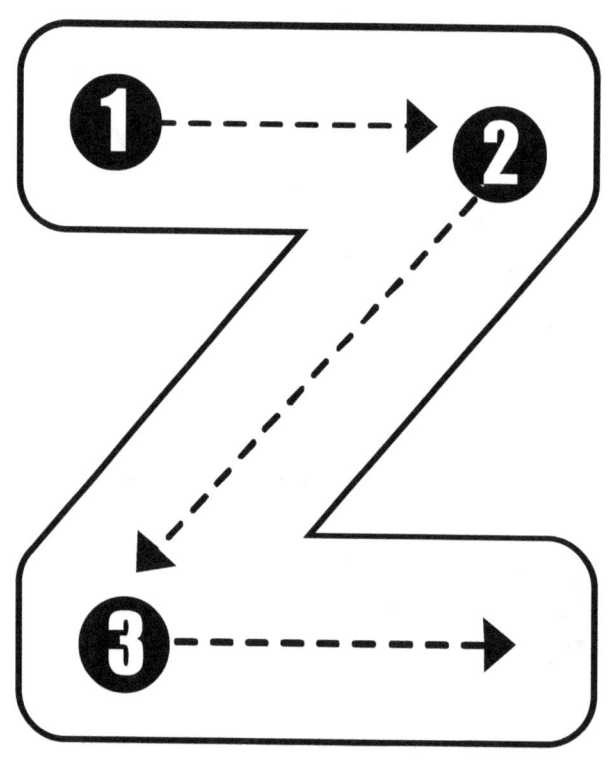

zebra

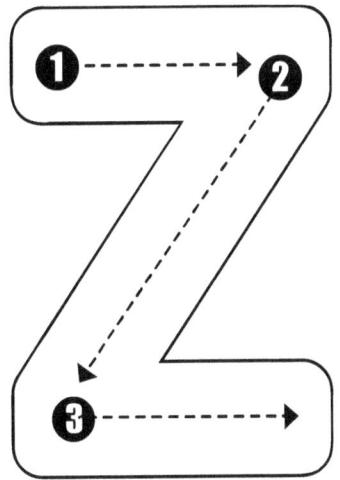 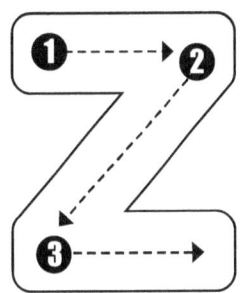
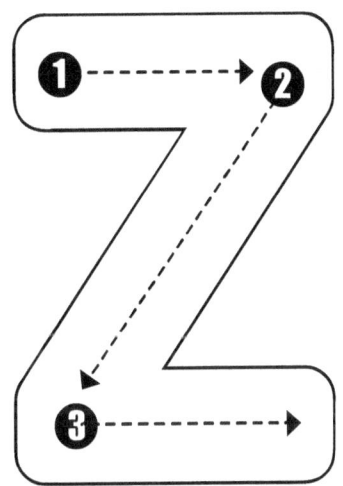 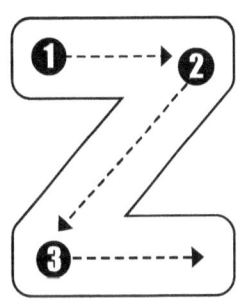
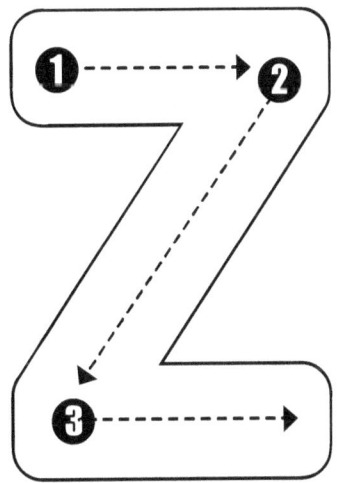 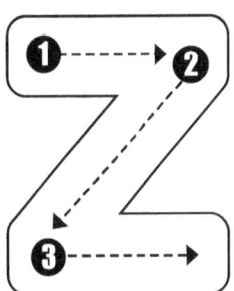

PART 3
NUMBERS

Trace with your finger and then with a crayon.

Start at

Follow the dotted line.

End at the arrowhead

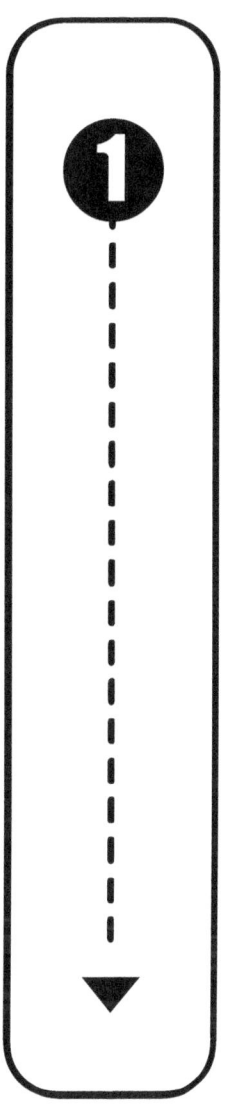

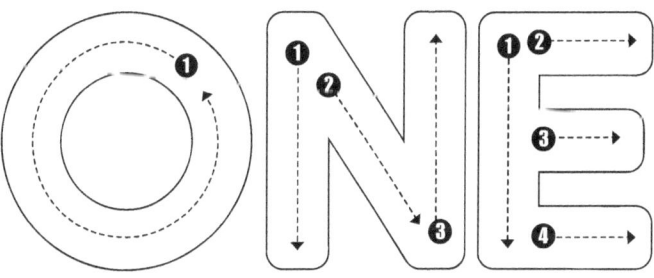

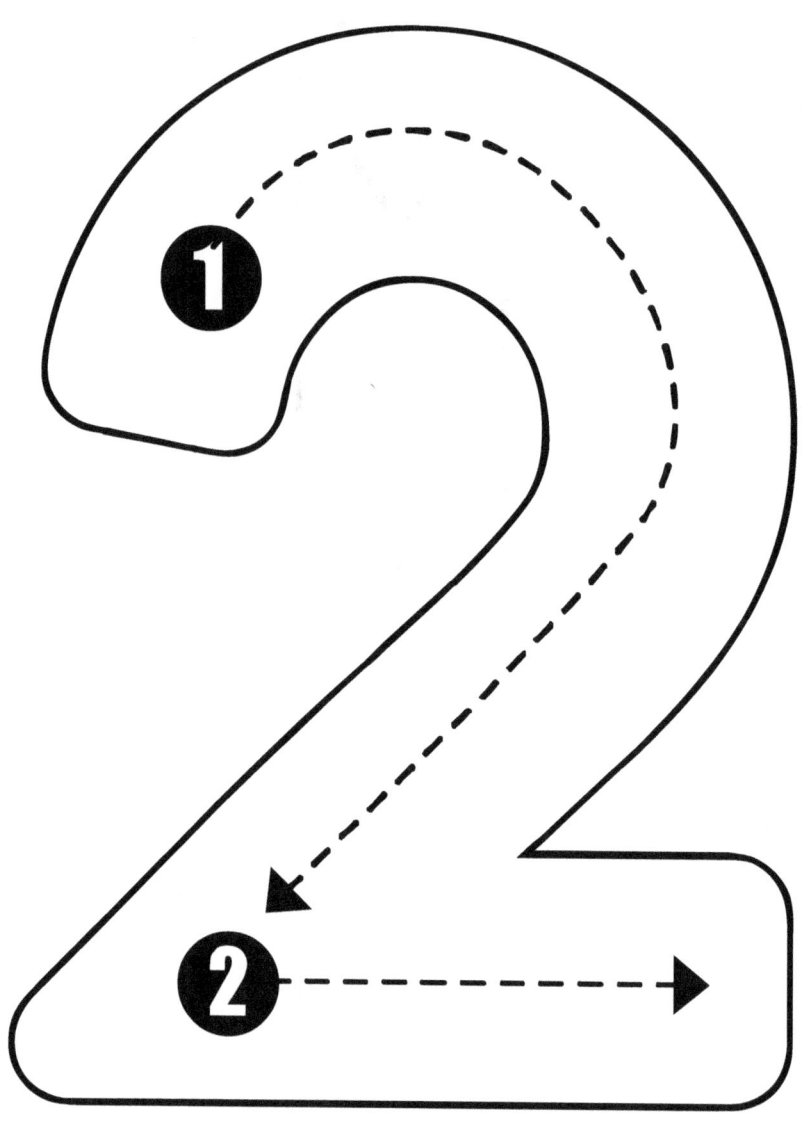

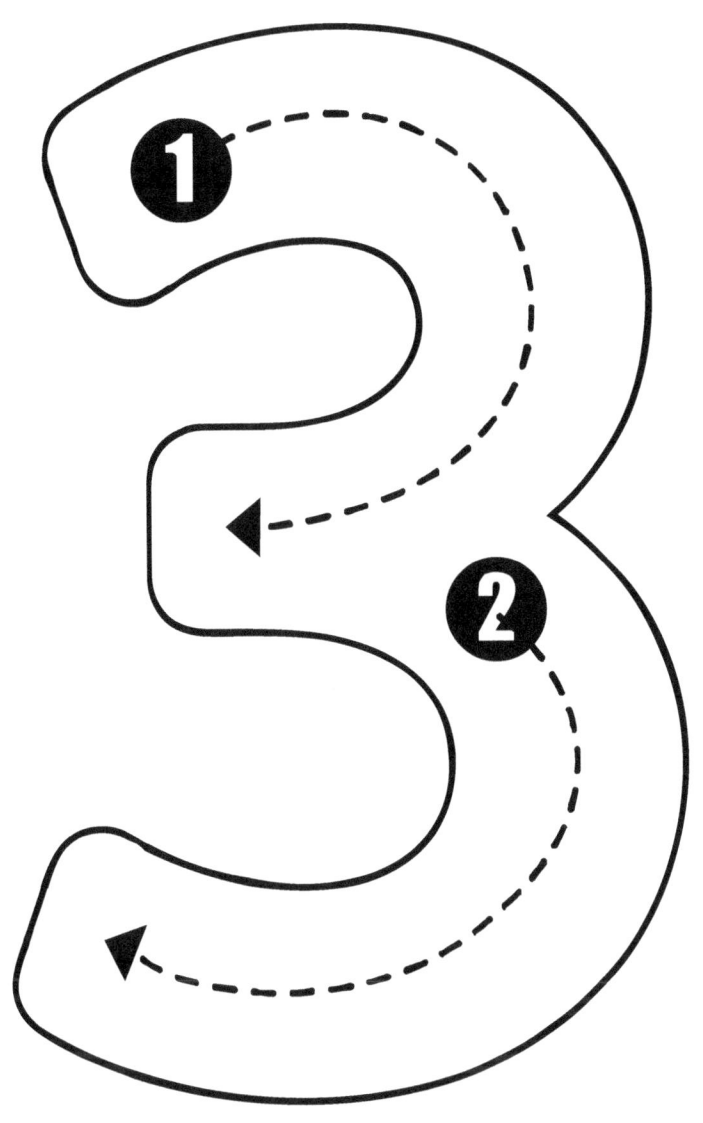

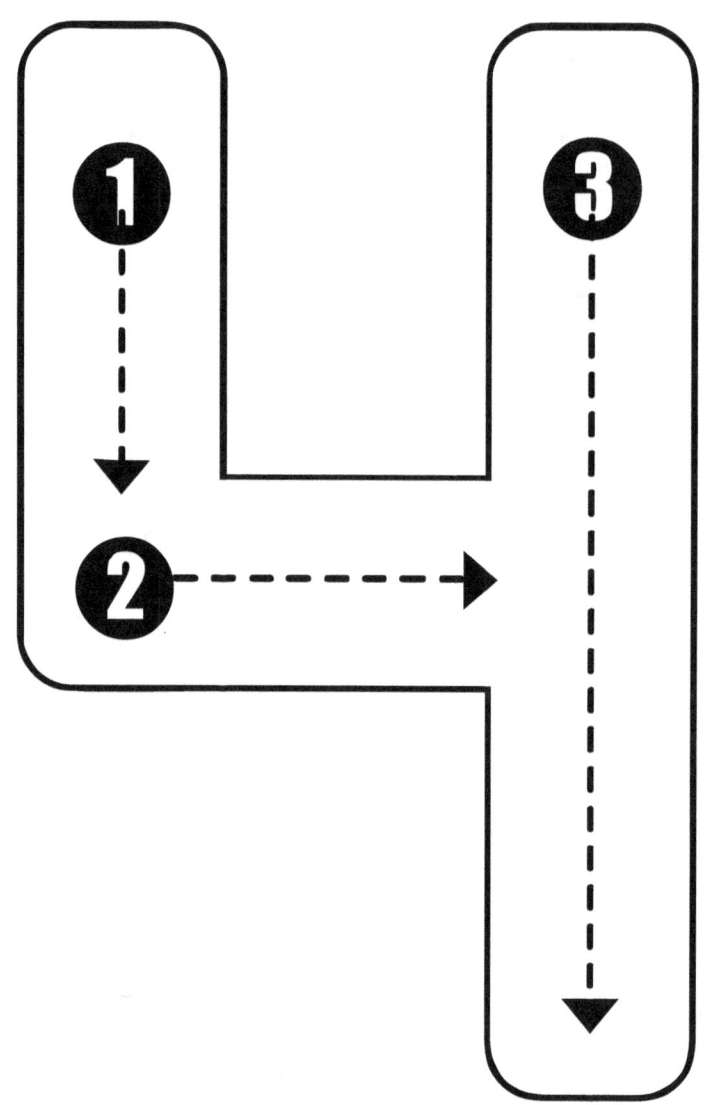

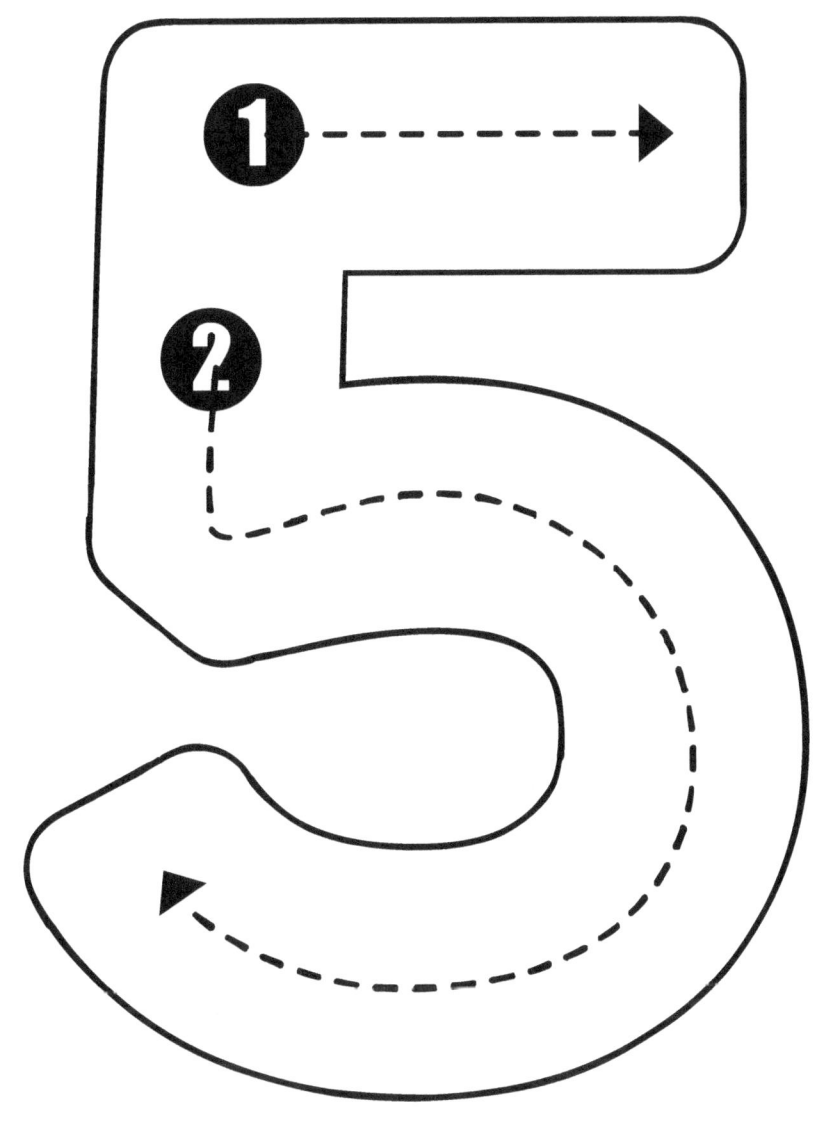
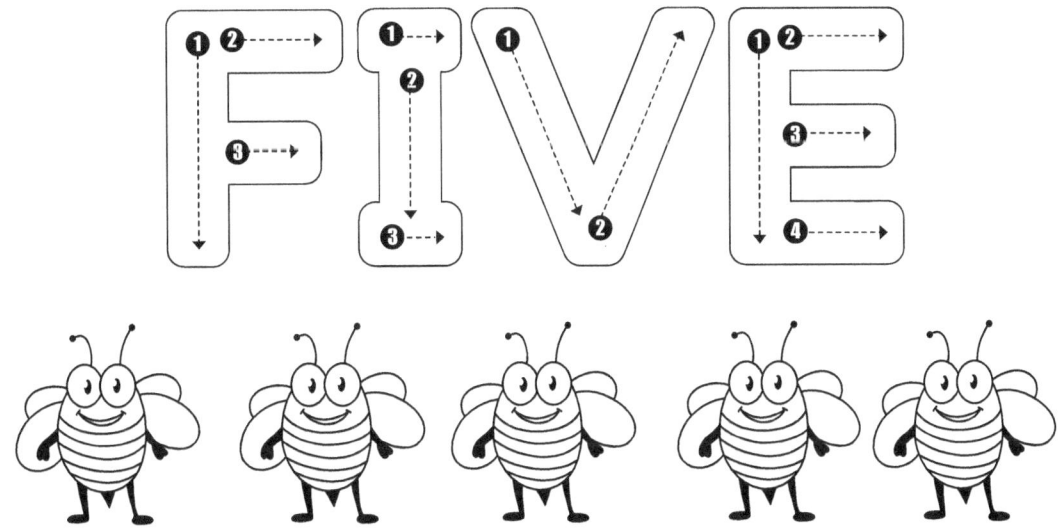

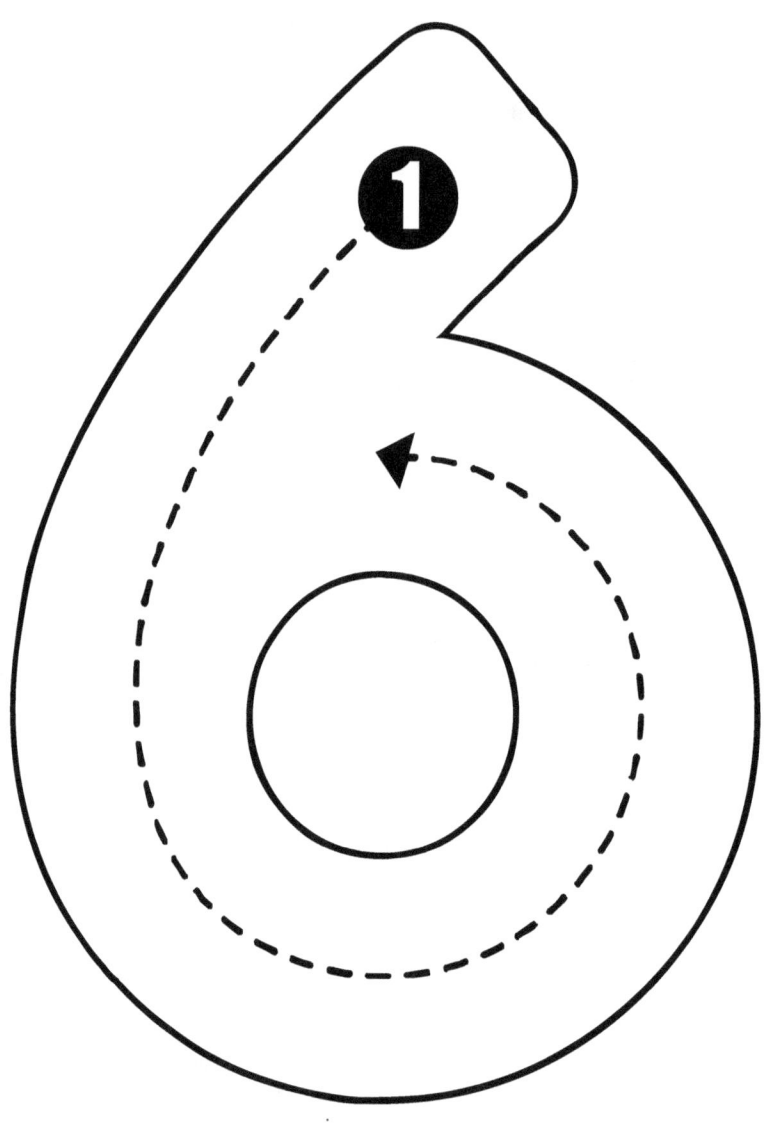

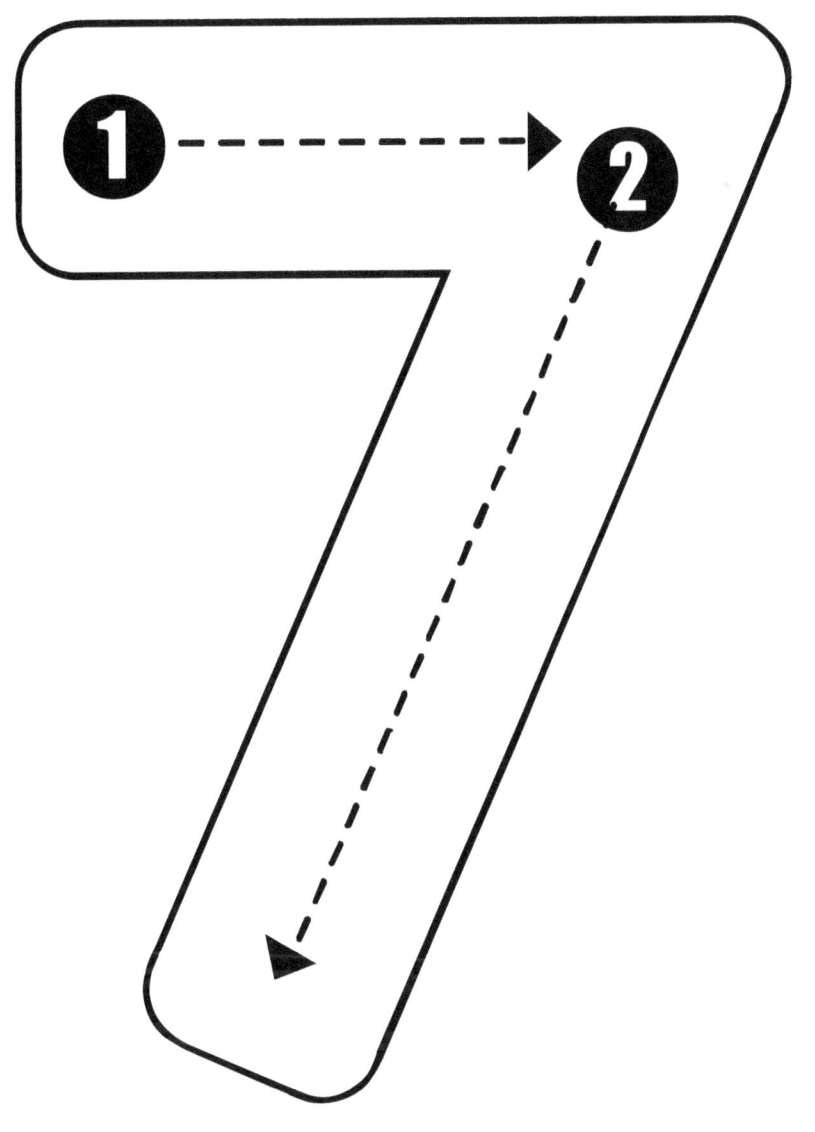
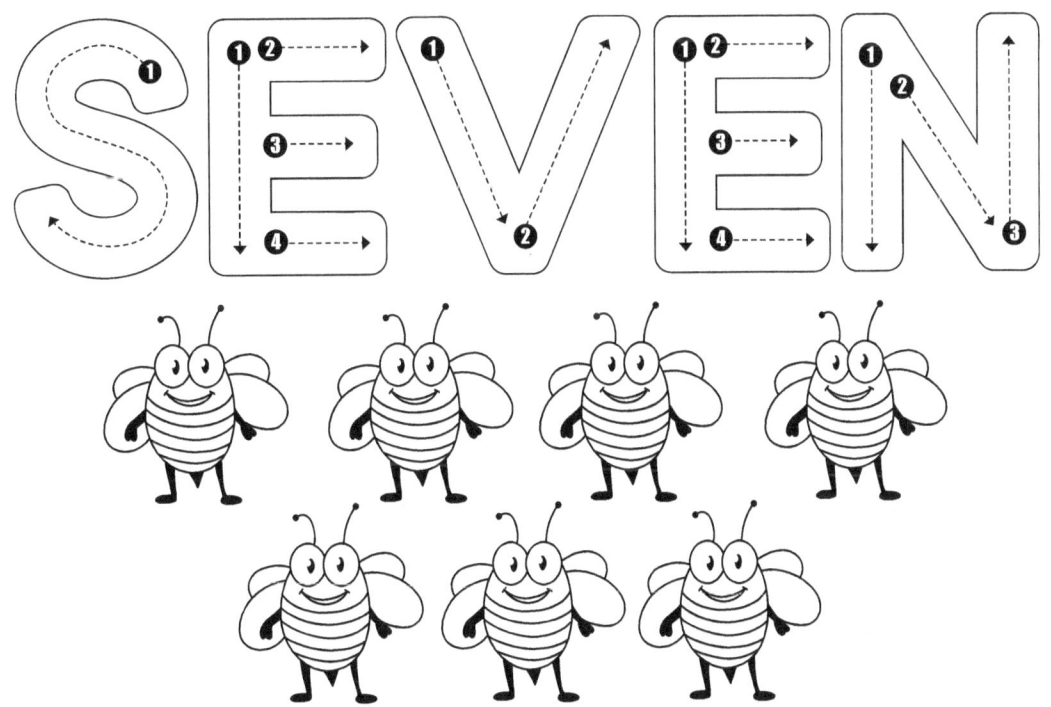

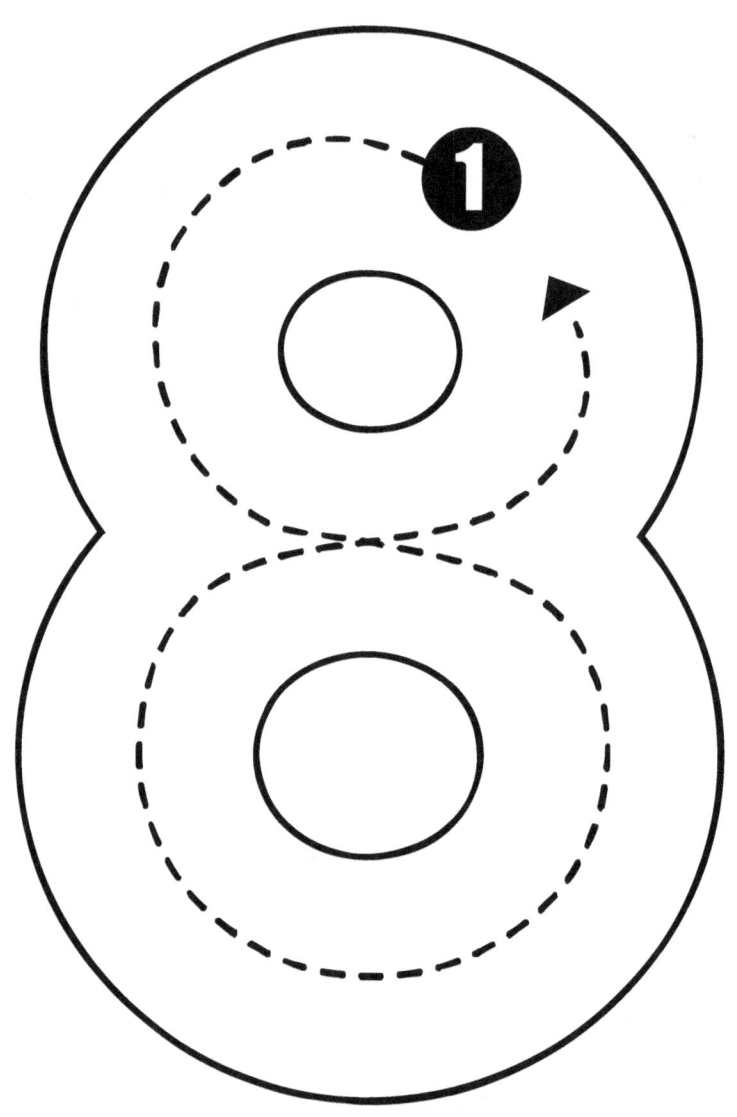

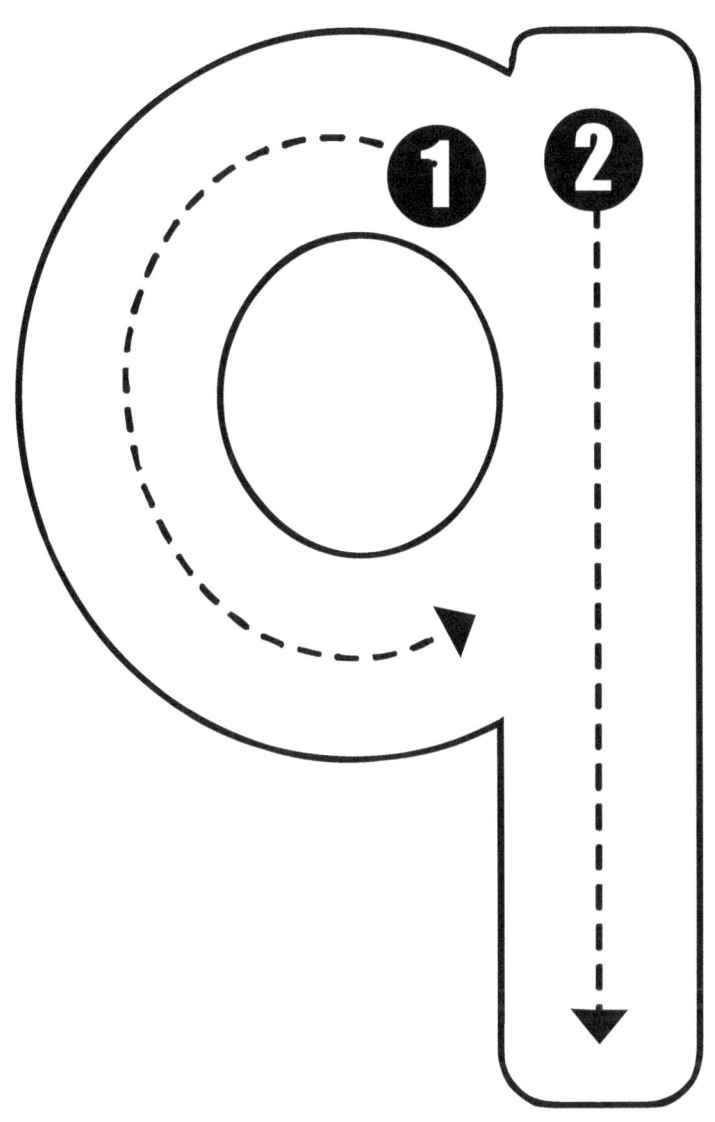

10

TEN

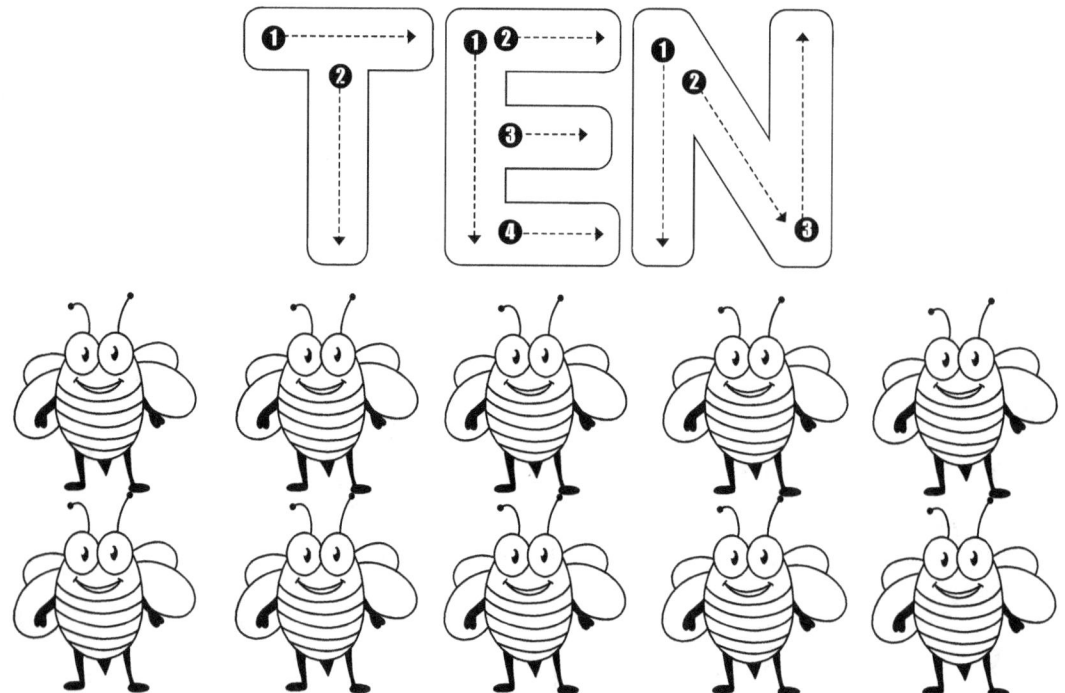

Congratulation on completing this workbook!

Don't forget to claim one of our free, ready-to-print certificates and reward your child's effort in completing our workbook. Access the link below or scan the QR code to get your free bonus! Fonts by Artsy Pantsy

https://mailchi.mp/12abf0326fc4/certificate-of-completion

SCAN ME

www.ingramcontent.com/pod-product-compliance
Lightning Source LLC
LaVergne TN
LVHW060203080526
838202LV00052B/4194